THE WAY OF LIFE

The Way of Life

A Theology of Christian Vocation

Gary D. Badcock

WILLIAM B. EERDMANS PUBLISHING COMPANY
GRAND RAPIDS, MICHIGAN / CAMBRIDGE, U.K.

© 1998 Wm. B. Eerdmans Publishing Co.
255 Jefferson Ave. S.E., Grand Rapids, Michigan 49503 /
P.O. Box 163, Cambridge CB3 9PU U.K.

Printed in the United States of America

03 02 01 00 99 98   7 6 5 4 3 2 1

Library of Congress Cataloging-in-Publication Data

Badcock, Gary D.
The way of life: a theology of Christian vocation / Gary D. Badcock.
p.   cm.
Includes bibliographical references and index.
ISBN 0-8028-4490-1 (pbk.: alk. paper)
1. Vocation — Christianity. I. Title.
BV4740.B23 1998
248.4 — dc21   98-28329
CIP

Unless otherwise noted, the Scripture quotations in this publication
are from the New Revised Standard Version Bible, copyright © 1989
by the Division of Christian Education of the National Council of
Churches of Christ in the U.S.A., and used by permission.

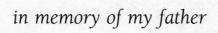
in memory of my father

Contents

vii

Contents

Acknowledgments

A number of people have assisted in writing this volume. My mother, first of all, hosted my family at her home in Newfoundland during my sabbatical leave from the University of Edinburgh in the spring and summer of 1996, when most of the writing was done. Two Scottish friends subsequently read the manuscript and made many useful suggestions and comments: Mrs. Elizabeth Candlish of St. Andrews, and the Rev. Dugald Cameron of St. Martin's Parish, The Church of Scotland, Edinburgh. The author, however, takes full responsibility for all views expressed. Another friend consented to allow a number of personal details to be included. And last, but by no means least, my wife Susan has to be thanked for her patience in enduring the birth-pangs of the author while awaiting her own, and for entertaining our eldest daughter more or less single-handedly as the book was written.

CHAPTER 1

Vocation and Christian Theology

Vocation as a Religious Question

Children raised in religious homes are often told that God has a plan for their lives. I was certainly such a child. During the course of my religious instruction, I heard not only that God has such a plan but also that I have freedom to discover and to follow this plan, and that my personal happiness, my "beatitude" to use the old theological term, depends to a great extent upon how well I follow it. Personal fulfillment has its goal, therefore, in the will of God for me. If I stray a little, no lasting damage may result; God is able to redeem even our mistakes and to use them for good. Should I rebel to such an extent as to damage myself or others more severely, however, then the happiness possible at the start may no longer be attainable. Dropping out of school at sixteen would certainly impair my chances in life. A bad marriage would hurt me deeply and would perhaps ruin me. But God gives guidance through the Bible, through the voice of conscience, through the advice of

1

another person, or perhaps through a book. If I listen and obey, his will can be done on earth, and because God is love, blessing will follow.

It was a simple and attractive vision of life, offering clear moral and religious meaning. Now that I am a grown man, however, and a theologian as well, there is much in it that I find perplexing. "When I was a child . . . I reasoned like a child; when I became an adult, I put an end to childish ways" (1 Cor. 13:11). Is divine providence really frustrated by human decision? Does God plot the ideal course of my life from all eternity, or does he make the story up as time goes on, adapting it to a situation that I myself help to create? How do I hear the voice of God? Is the moral good constituted solely by the will of God? The questions run deep, raising fundamental religious and theological issues, and they can readily be multiplied. Does God give me natural gifts that he expects me to use in his service, and ought this to affect my choice of a career? Or is God's will as often as not something opposed to inclination and even to natural aptitude? At his call to become a prophet, Jeremiah complained that he did not know how to speak; the Lord was obliged to "put out his hand" and touch him, so putting his words into the prophet's mouth (Jer. 1:4-9). Is a genuine "calling" always like this, so that God's work necessarily requires some supernatural endowment to fulfill?

Not all of such questions can be addressed in this short book. The difficult theoretical problem of providence and divine action in particular lies well beyond its scope. Our purpose is more basic, if rather less ambitious: it is to try to locate the concept of vocation in a theological framework, in order to shed light on it as a religious concept. The intention, therefore, is primarily to speak to religious need and not to address theoretical concerns, although along the way it will be necessary to draw fairly extensively on a range of theological scholarship.

Underlying everything that follows is a conviction developed over the years that the question of vocation is often the basic *religious* question that people ask: "What will I do with my life?" or "What will I do with the rest of my life?" It is not just that people tend to define others by their work, or that they also tend to identify themselves by reference to what they do. It is true that identity is closely related to the working roles we assume. But identity is also, at root, a religious matter, for the question "Who am I?" is only finally answerable in the light of one's wider moral goals, one's worldview, and one's sense of the "meaning of life." The question "Who am I?" is thus inseparable from another: "Who *ought* I to be?" Such questions are much more fundamental to the religious quest than those that usually preoccupy the theologians and preachers; for example, "Is there a God?" is a valid enough question to ask — and one that has an obvious bearing on the question of vocation — but it is not itself the central question. The central question is what this might mean *for me,* what bearing it has on life, what it entails for human existence generally and for the particular human existence of the one who poses the question in the first place.

Vocation in the Bible

Vocation means "calling" (from the Latin *vocare,* "to call"), and in the Bible, the call comes from God. Language about the divine call is common in the Bible. The Hebrew verb "to call" (קרע) is one of the more frequently occurring words in the Old Testament. It is often closely associated with "election" (בחר), as in Isaiah 41:8-9, but the semantic ranges of the two words are distinct. The call refers to a personal or collective summons by God, whereas election is the deliberate act of God in choosing someone to share in his saving purposes. The

3

difference might be summed up by saying that human beings experience divine election in their call, while the call has its basis in election.

In the Old Testament, therefore, the call of God is restricted to those whom he has chosen, his people Israel. But within these limits, the call can have several distinct senses. The most general is the call to repentance, whether collective or individual. The Old Testament abounds in passages in which God calls upon his people to repent and to be renewed (e.g., Jer. 3:12ff.). The word itself, however, is more often used in connection with a specific call to some personal office, as in the case of the Servant in Isaiah 42:6: "I am the LORD, I have called you in righteousness, I have taken you by the hand and kept you; I have given you as a covenant to the people, a light to the nations." Such a call can be intensely personal, as for the prophet Samuel who heard the voice of God as a little child, "Samuel! Samuel!" (1 Sam. 3:4ff.). God thus calls people "by name" (Isa. 43:1; 45:3). In the Old Testament, the call also serves as a metaphor for God's initiative in the lives of the patriarchs, and thus, implicitly, in the life of the whole nation descended from them. While the word "call" does not feature in the patriarchal narratives themselves, it later comes to be used of them, in particular in Second Isaiah: "Listen to me, O Jacob, and Israel, whom I called" (Isa. 48:12); or "Look to Abraham your father and to Sarah who bore you; for he was but one when I called him, but I blessed him and made him many" (Isa. 51:2). On the strength of this, contemporary translations of the Bible use headings such as "The Call of Abram" to describe the contents of a passage such as Genesis 12:1-9, even though the word "call" only came to be used of it later.

In the New Testament, the Greek verb "to call" ($\varkappa\alpha\lambda\tilde{\epsilon}\tilde{\iota}\nu$) appears frequently again, reflecting the Old Testament precedent. The fundamental usage is Jesus' own: "I have come to call not the righteous but sinners" (Mark 2:17). The idea of the call here denotes Jesus' very mission: his purpose is "to call" to repentance and discipleship, while his insistence on associating with the disreputable and the sinner in issuing the call leads to conflict with the more conventionally "religious," in this case the "scribes of the Pharisees" (Mark 2:16). Jesus calls people to follow him in his ministry, so much so that a whole New Testament genre can be discerned in the collected call stories. In the synoptic Gospels, all discipleship is presented as the result of Jesus' personal calling; there is no instance of anyone volunteering successfully to become a disciple.[1] It seems, rather, that Jesus' summons has a literally miraculous effect on those called, as his unconditional demand is met freely with an instant response: "As he went a little farther, he saw James son of Zebedee and his brother John, who were in their boat mending the nets. Immediately he called them; and they left their father Zebedee in the boat with the hired men, and followed him" (Mark 1:19-20).

Elsewhere in the New Testament, it is not Christ but God who generally calls. With God as the subject, however, the word and its derivatives can actually serve as technical terms for salvation, or for some function in bringing salvation about. This is especially true of Paul's writings. Paul is called to be an apostle (1 Cor. 1:1), but more usually the call is to salvation and to its ethical implications (e.g., 1 Cor. 1:2; 1:24). An interesting usage appears in 2 Timothy 1:8-9: "relying on the power of God, who saved us and called us with a holy calling, not according to our works but according to his own purpose and grace." It is unclear what this call "with a holy calling" means, but "to a holy calling" is also a grammatical possibility (cf. "to a holy life," NIV), in which case the phrase refers either

---

1. So A. J. Drodge, "Call Stories," *The Anchor Bible Dictionary* (New York: Doubleday, 1992), vol. 1, p. 821.

to the apostolic ministry or else to the general Christian calling to holiness. This expression, however, is not typically Pauline.

Thus far, then, there is no suggestion that a biblical "calling" has reference to any secular mode of life or to any form of employment. There is, in fact, only one possible exception to this in the whole of the New Testament, found in 1 Corinthians 7:17-24:

> let each one of you lead the life that the Lord has assigned, to which God called you. This is my rule in all the churches. Was anyone at the time of his call already circumcised? Let him not seek to remove the marks of circumcision. . . . Were you a slave when called? Do not be concerned about it. . . . In whatever condition you were called, brothers and sisters, there remain with God.

This is an important text — indeed, a crucial one, for upon it rests the whole attempt to argue from the Bible that one's *work* can be a *vocation* in the strict theological sense. Two key expressions are used here; the first is the phrase "to which God has called you" of verse 17, as the New Revised Standard Version translates the text, which seems to suggest in this context that a "calling" can include one's racial or religious identity (the case of a Jewish Christian), or alternatively one's socioeconomic status (the case of the believing slave). The Greek text, however, is obscure: the key clause reads ἕκαστον ὡς κέκληκεν ὁ θεός, which translated literally reads, "each one as God has called." In its context, this is almost certainly once again to be rendered differently than we find in the NRSV. The Jerusalem Bible is much nearer the mark when it more freely translates the verse as follows: "what each one has is what the Lord has given him and he should continue as he was when God's call reached him." Here the sense of the "call" is the same as elsewhere in the Pauline writings — indeed, in the whole of the Bible: the summons to faith, obedience, and salvation that is so basic to the Word of God.

The second key expression, however, is the clause in verse 20 that reads in the NRSV, "In whatever condition you were called." The Greek is more direct: ἕκαστος ἐν τῇ κλήσει ᾗ ἐκλήθη, which translated literally reads, "each one in the calling in which he was called." Here at last, it seems, is evidence of occupation as vocation. One commentator states:

> The calling in which he was called bears a double significance of the term "call." The calling in which one is to remain must refer to what one was doing occupationally at the time of conversion. Whatever it was, Paul dignifies it by designating it a calling. The second "call," the passive form, refers evidently to the call of the gospel through which one became a Christian. The first calling is not to be negated or necessarily changed by the second.[2]

C. K. Barrett, in his superb commentary on the epistle, is more explicit: one is not called to a new occupation; rather, one's old occupation is given new significance; the calling in verse 20 is not the calling "*with* which, *to* which, or *by* which a man is called, but refers to the state in which he is *when* he is called by God to become a Christian."[3] A noted exegete from an older generation, James Moffatt, postulates that Paul's thought at this point is analogous to Stoic moral philosophy: if one has inner freedom, one need not mind one's outward condition.[4]

2. William F. Orr and James Arthur Walther, *1 Corinthians* (Garden City: Doubleday, 1976), p. 216.

3. C. K. Barrett, *A Commentary on the First Epistle to the Corinthians* (London: Adam & Charles Black, 1968), pp. 169-70.

4. James Moffatt, *The First Epistle of Paul to the Corinthians* (London: Hodder and Stoughton, 1938), pp. 85-87.

On closer examination, however, the equation of "calling" with "occupation" appears questionable even here. For Paul at no point actually speaks of *employment* in the text. His point, rather, relates to one's condition in life; indeed, in the passage under consideration, only circumcision and uncircumcision are actually mentioned, neither of which has any direct connection with the question of occupation. The whole context of the passage is also important to remember; the discussion of calling follows a lengthy treatment of whether or not the believer should marry and the situation of the believer who is married to an unbeliever. Paul's purpose seems to be to resist the idea that the new life of the Christian entails an upheaval in the social, legal, and racial spheres. In verse 21, the condition of the slave is introduced: "Were you a slave when called?" This is as close as we come to an identification of occupation with calling in the chapter, but even here there is nothing to suggest that such an identification was really in Paul's mind. Moffatt's reference to Stoic moral thought is, in fact, much more apposite.

Biblical language, then, differs markedly from much contemporary usage. In the secular world, one's "calling" or "vocation" has come to mean simply "occupation," particularly in the professions. This is especially true of American English. In *Time* magazine, for example, one can find endless examples of such language; one of the more anachronistic appeared in the April 12 edition of 1993, when Robert Hughes, writing of the Venetian artist Giorgio da Castelfranco, described "the exquisite portrait of a young knight surrounded by the gleaming black weapons of his vocation." Unfortunately, no knight of the late Italian Renaissance would have conceived of his life as a "vocation," for in the Middle Ages this was a term used exclusively to denote the religious life. Priests and religious had vocations; knights did not.

Later, we shall need to ask the question whether the

8

medieval or the modern understanding comes closer to the biblical concept of vocation. For the present, however, we may note that use of the word *calling* in the Bible does not appear to support the naive vision of the Christian life with which this book, and indeed much of my own early religious training, began. This may come as something of a surprise; it may even be disturbing to the young Christian seeking a sense of direction in career choices to hear that the Bible is (to this extent at least) silent on the whole matter. But if we are to take our lead from the language of Scripture, then we will do well to consider carefully whether the concept of vocation can quite so readily be extended to the question of secular employment. On the other hand, this does not of itself mean that there is *no* sense in which questions of religious vocation enter the sphere of work. What we can and must say at the outset, however, is that at best one's work can be understood as a vocation only in a derivative and secondary sense.

In fact, this provides a useful starting place for a theology of vocation. First of all, it clears the ground for us, and such a clearing away is often the first step needed in any new development. Nothing can impede the dawn of new understanding quite so effectively as a conflicting set of preconceived ideas. Second, the sense of the word *calling* in the Bible offers a helpful corrective to a certain tendency in some Christian piety — including that of my youth — to see each mundane detail of life as of supreme importance to God, as if one were required to seek his will in every detail. Whatever the heavenly blueprint may contain, the decision whether to do the shopping in the morning or in the afternoon is unlikely to be among its features. Perhaps, then, we ought to say the same of the decision between becoming a mechanic and becoming a postal worker. In the Bible, after all, the Christian calling refers to the reorientation of human life to God through repentance, faith, and obedience; to participation in God's saving purpose in history; and to the

9

heavenly goal: "I press on toward the goal for the prize of the heavenly call of God in Christ Jesus" (Phil. 3:14). Thus the first step in coming to a proper understanding of one's vocation is to see that it is defined by such openly theological criteria. The Christian calling is nothing less than to love God and one's neighbor, as Jesus teaches — or alternatively, to respond to the Word of grace with faith and obedience, to use a more characteristically Pauline expression. It is, in other words, to live the Christian life. This must always be the substance of the doctrine of vocation — and the core of our answer to the question "What will I do with my life?"

Work and Human Dignity

Nevertheless, Christian theology must recognize the value of work in human society and in individual lives. This is especially so because of the moral dimension implicit in all work and explicit in much of it. It is by work that human life progresses: work in the home, on the land and the sea, in factories and schools, in government, and even in the church has the potential to bring material, social, and spiritual well-being to people. Without these varieties of work, human society as we know it would be inconceivable. Work, therefore, is something more than just a natural necessity. It is, rather, something that befits human dignity. As Pope John Paul II has written: "Work is a good thing for man — a good thing for his humanity — because through work man not only transforms nature, adapting it to his own needs, but he also achieves fulfilment as a human being and indeed in a sense becomes 'more a human being.'"[5]

The positive possibilities of work are clear; and since work

5. John Paul II, *Laborem exercens,* English translation in *Origins* 11 (24 September 1981): 40.

is basic to human existence, it is a perennial human concern. For example, in *Utopia,* his classic work of political philosophy, St. Thomas More described an ideal society, one of the more prominent features of which is that it contains no unemployment or purposelessness. Each person in the utopia applies himself or herself to a chosen trade, in addition to which all work in some capacity in agriculture. Because everyone is engaged in practical activity, there is plenty for all, for there is no idleness either at the top or bottom of the social order. For the same reason, More tells us, labor can be confined to six hours in the day, the rest being left free for other worthwhile things. No worker is ever "wearied like a beast of burden with constant toil from early morning till late at night."[6] Periods of activity are punctuated by times of rest, recreation, and education. The goal is a total life in which the citizen achieves happiness in the context of peace and freedom from the tyranny of greed and want alike. It is a dreamlike world, but though *Utopia* was first published in 1516, directed to an English audience under Henry VIII, its essential vision still appeals to us, for here is a *humane* social order directed to the good of each and all, in which the abilities of every individual are harnessed to a constructive end.

There is no suggestion that More seriously believed that such a social order was a practical possibility. The point was more modest: to set up a theoretical standard by which to judge the prevailing corruption of the political order and to outline the contours of a different model of collective life. Too much has taken place in subsequent centuries for us ever to believe that More's "new world order" is a more practicable option now than it was when first proposed. His is, for example, a primitive communist vision, something not uncommon among Christian

6. St. Thomas More, *Utopia,* ed. Edward Surtz (New Haven and London: Yale University Press, 1964), p. 69.

humanists; but the history of the twentieth century leaves us generally ill-disposed toward communism — certainly in its Marxist and Stalinist varieties. His insistence upon the simple virtues of agriculture is also jarring to the modern mind: everyone in utopia, it seems, is a part-time farmer. It is true that people today often yearn nostalgically for a return to the land and are frequently highly "committed" to nature through their awareness of environmental issues. But mechanization and urbanization make the more fully blown agrarian quality of More's utopianism inconceivable for us. Even in a country like Canada, for which agriculture is an extremely important industry, only about seven percent of the population has any direct connection with the land.

At one point, however, we can still make common cause with More's utopian dream: the ideal world is one in which all have a productive role to play. In our own day, we have become all too aware of an alternative possibility, a world in which the great goals become corporate "downsizing" and efficiency gains at any human cost. These have brought upon us massive uncertainty in the workplace and despair in the queues of the unemployed. As recently as 1957, an Anglican writer could speak of the overcoming of mass unemployment in Britain as the great achievement of the *Christian* social vision carved out amid the hardship of the 1930s and claim that large-scale economic exploitation and poverty were, as a result, no longer significant social evils.[7] Unfortunately, one could not say the same today, for forty years later mass unemployment and mass poverty have risen grotesquely in Britain, and indeed throughout the Western world. The situation is even worse in Russia and other Eastern European countries after the collapse of communism.

This is not a book about economics, the morality of work,

7. Harry Blamires, *The Will and the Way* (London: SPCK, 1957), p. 72.

or the immorality of poverty, but about vocation as a theological concept. Nevertheless, it would be well to remind ourselves at the outset that for a great many people in our time the whole discussion is likely to have a hollow sound to it, particularly because of the popular associations of the word *vocation*. What sense does it make to speak to someone of this if there is for him or her virtually no possibility of finding dignity in work? And if there is no work, if the skills that become necessary for some simply to survive are the skills of the professional burglar or prostitute or the skill to extract every available penny from the social security system, how much can we finally blame those who turn to such things for a living? One of the traditional questions posed in moral theology is whether the starving child who steals an apple is guilty of a crime. Many theologians have replied in the negative: no, the child is neither a criminal nor a sinner. On the grander scale, though perhaps with an awareness of greater ambiguity, the same question can be asked again, and no doubt in some cases an analogous answer can be given.

Against such a background, however, perhaps the concept of vocation has a uniquely important role to play. It is a concept that reflects something of human dignity in the moral sphere. The concept of vocation itself is possible and meaningful, not only because there is a God who calls, but also because there are human beings who are capable of good things, of love and fidelity, of faith and service, as much as they are capable of achieving concrete, practical roles in life as plumbers or parents or pastors. To live a full human life in this sense — this is what the concept of vocation involves, so that the denial of vocation means the denial of one's own humanity and the leading of a less than human life. This is the idea that we shall seek to explore in what follows in this book.

CHAPTER 2

Faith and Work

Approaches to God

When asked by one of the scribes which was the greatest
commandment, Jesus answered, "you shall love the Lord your
God with all your heart, and with all your soul, and with all
your mind, and with all your strength" (Mark 12:30 par.; Deut.
6:5). This statement, and its corollary in the commandment
"You shall love your neighbor as yourself" (Mark 12:31 par.;
Lev. 19:18), serves not only as evidence of Jesus' interpretation
of the Jewish moral law, and as a summary of his positive ethical
teaching, but also as the key to a proper understanding of his
own mission. Jesus himself is a man who stands for God and
his neighbor. What he does during his ministry is nothing other
than the will of God as outlined in these two great commandments. Much of his teaching, furthermore, is intended to draw
the two together, to show that one cannot love God unless one
also loves one's neighbor. On this question, the Fourth Gospel
and the Epistles of John are totally consistent with the witness
of Matthew, Mark, and Luke. Supremely, Jesus' death on the
cross is at once his own total obedience to the will of the Father

and his total solidarity with his neighbor. In Jesus we have the ultimate paradigm for how the two dimensions of love, the vertical and the horizontal, are really one.

It is a risky business to take a statement such as Mark 12:30, which makes mention of the human heart, soul, mind, and strength, as if it served as a kind of map of the self, outlining the human psychological faculties. Nevertheless, this much at least is of interest and importance. Whereas much traditional theological anthropology has been dualist (body and soul), and whereas some of it has been tripartite (following the body, soul, and spirit terminology of 1 Thess. 5:23), Jesus here speaks of four levels of the love of God within the self. The exegesis of this text is admittedly difficult, not least because of variations in the relevant texts. The Old Testament source speaks of only the heart, soul, and strength, while Matthew's version of the story lists the heart, soul, and mind (Matt. 22:37). Luke, for its part, speaks of the heart, soul, strength, and mind (10:27), but the words are those of the scribe rather than of Jesus and are found in a totally different context in the gospel, preceding the parable of the good Samaritan. The sense of the word *soul* is also controversial, in particular because of the transition made from a Hebraic to a Greek context in the move from the Old to the New Testament. What is clear, however, is that the words amount to more than a series of synonyms for the same thing, and that the point is to call men and women to love God with the whole self, involving all their human capabilities and energies.

The word *vocation* in the broadest sense is one that corresponds to all of these, for the fundamental human vocation is to do the will of God. That will, however, is what is revealed in Holy Scripture, and in a particularly concise way in the texts just cited. This wider context, as we have already seen, must always serve as the framework for the whole concept. To the extent that we can speak more narrowly of vocation as a concrete mode of life, however, in the sense that one's life work can be a moral and spiritual project, then no doubt it is the word *strength* in Mark 12:30 that corresponds most closely to it. One's strength here denotes more than simply physical strength or natural ability. It brings into focus human energy and the whole practical side of the reality of human existence. We are, among other things, embodied beings for whom physical action is something meaningful. The physical, in fact, can already be for us something "spiritual," as in the case of the work of art or the religious symbol, and most of all in the case of moral action. In fact, if the claims of morality are to be taken seriously, then such action is perhaps the most meaningful and spiritual thing of all. To serve God with one's strength is to do the will of God in this everyday sense, in action and deed rather than merely in theory. There is really no such thing as an "armchair Christian."

This by no means implies that action is the sum of all that is meaningful or that meaning is always practical. The intellectual love of God is still, I would argue, a possibility — indeed, it is a necessity according to Mark 12:30. But the point is to locate action, and the whole practical sphere of human existence, at the center of things rather than at the periphery. In this way, the practical side of the concept of vocation can be seen as a fundamental dimension of the human response to God, rather than something peripheral or derivative. Vocation is best understood in terms of this basic tenet of theology, that humanity is called by God to faith, to holiness, and to service.

One of the merits of the recently published *Catechism of the Catholic Church* is that it begins with precisely this theme — not with God or with the Scriptures, but with the idea of the supernatural calling of humanity to share the life of God. Obviously, belief in God and the deposit of Scripture and a host of attendant doctrines of the Christian faith are presupposed from the beginning, but it is nevertheless refreshing to find the concept of vocation at the head and heart of what follows. The opening paragraph begins:

> God, infinitely perfect and blessed in himself, in a plan of sheer goodness freely created man to make him share in his own blessed life. For this reason, at every time and in every place, God draws close to man. He calls man to seek him, to know him, to love him with all his strength.[1]

It is in keeping with this calling and for its sake that the church exists, for the function of the church, the *Catechism* continues, is to proclaim the good news of how God has accomplished his good purpose through the coming of Christ, through the gift of the Spirit, and through the establishment of the church (I.2).

Earlier this century, the Catholic philosopher Jacques Maritain outlined a series of "approaches to God" in a book with that title — approaches ranging from what he calls the "primordial" or "pre-philosophical" knowledge of God possessed by the ordinary man or woman through the evidence afforded by our experience of the world (following Paul in Romans 1–2) through to a variety of ancient and modern versions of philosophical theism. He concludes his discussion, however, with a treatment of the ways by which the "practical intellect" apprehends God.[2] The awareness of beauty is included here, for Maritain insists that there is an enigmatic openness to the absolute beauty of God in all the more mundane experiences of the beautiful. Nevertheless, the practical

---

1. *Catechism of the Catholic Church* (New York: Doubleday, 1995), I.1.
2. Jacques Maritain, *Approches de Dieu,* in Jacques and Raïsa Maritain, *Oeuvres Complète* (Fribourg: Éditions Universitaires; Paris: Éditions Saint-Paul, 1982-), vol. 10 (1985), pp. 71ff.

apprehension of God finds expression supremely in the moral life. Maritain, as might be expected of a Catholic philosopher, holds that there can be no real justification for moral value apart from belief in God, but this moral-metaphysical point is not his primary emphasis. Rather, he argues that in the initial choice of the good which arises from human freedom — in the child, for example — God is present in an unconscious, non-conceptual, and oftentimes nonexplicit way. The choice of the good for the sake of the good alone, Maritain argues, is always a theological event, even when made by the avowed atheist. The good, in other words, is something transcendent, something absolute, and thus — implicitly at least — something divine. The denial of this in explicit philosophical systems of morality merely leads, as he puts it, to a "cadaver or an idol of the good" rather than to the thing itself. Very few have the courage to live with this. Practically, therefore, there are only pseudo-atheists.

We need not necessarily agree with Maritain's concept of the good, or with his doctrine of moral choice, in order to agree with him nonetheless that it may be possible to have a practical and perhaps also a preconscious relationship with God when at the theoretical level all is doubt or darkness. For we know only too well that the converse can happen, that one can know all the right things at the conscious level, or in theory, and yet fail to show that one truly "knows" God by one's actions. This is the sin of the hypocrite, but hypocrisy has a mirror opposite in the genuine goodness that we see in many people who are without any attachment to the truth as conceived and believed in an explicit religious faith. Implicit faith is to be preferred to explicit hypocrisy, of course, but the better alternative to both is sanctity with truth — "orthopraxy" (right action) with "orthodoxy" (right belief), to use one of the standard idioms of contemporary theological parlance. Only thus can one love the Lord God with the whole self.

18

Action and Meaning

There has been a strong tendency in recent Western thought to see all meaning as a function of practical activity. "Meaning as use" is a principle common to a variety of twentieth-century philosophical systems. It has been particularly prominent in what is sometimes generically called "postmodernism." Postmodern thought defines itself against what it sees as the over-rationalizing tendencies of the Western tradition, especially as seen in the Enlightenment, and prefers to see truth and value as contextual, practical constructs that enable humans to live together in community. This whole field is bewilderingly complex, but we may take the thought of one of its most important and influential thinkers, Jürgen Habermas, as representative. According to Habermas, "communicative action" is fundamental to human existence, for it is the means by which human societal life is achieved.[3] Society functions on the basis of some shared understanding, a culture of shared norms and ideals, but this shared culture has its real roots in action. To reach mutual understanding always presupposes a set of linguistic, concrete *acts* on the part of those who meet in dialogue. Mutual understanding can be expressed either in terms of truth or in social or ethical norms, but in either case the ruling idea is consensus. Truth or value is what enables a pragmatic goal to be attained: life together, which is fundamentally a practical rather than a theoretical or a moral goal in the strict sense.

Postmodern thought of this sort has been taken up extensively in recent theology. The claim is that the life of the church provides the pragmatic goal for the sake of which theology exists, and that its worship and service constitute the practical context within which its statements make sense and legitimate

3. The key source is Jürgen Habermas, *The Theory of Communicative Action,* trans. T. McCarthy, 2 vols. (Boston: Beacon Press, 1983).

themselves. If, in other words, all human truth or value claims are radically contextual and derive their authority, not from some independent criterion, but solely from the function they have in some human community, then theological statements are legitimated by the church, since the life of the church is as valid a form of human community as any other. Thus, though Habermas himself is critical of religion, postmodern theologians have argued that his criticism of religion cannot be sustained and that in fact his philosophy tends to support religious life. Since religion "creates community and establishes identity," its claim to a role in the ongoing conversation of communicative reason is as secure as that of any other participant.[4]

My own view is that Habermas rather than the theologians has reached the more consistent conclusion at this point: if "meaning is use," to paraphrase the position again, then religion obviously becomes something highly questionable. The reason lies in what might be described as the "totalizing" tendencies of religion, which stem from its belief in God, or in the ultimate, conceived as existing transcendently to the world. This is clearly, and one might say self-evidently, something more than a "communicative praxis." In fact, the whole postmodern experiment in contemporary thought presupposes the extinction of all such thought in the cultural death of God. To my mind, this makes postmodern philosophy per se the enemy of religion and therefore severely limits its usefulness as a tool for the theologian.

For theology, therefore, meaning cannot lie in use alone. Theology must insist, rather, upon the old idea that it is God who gives meaning, creatively and redemptively. It must therefore resist all attempts to argue that meaning is a purely human construct, a this-worldly, provisional, and practical reality

4. Edmund Arens, *Christopraxis: A Theology of Action*, trans. John F. Hoffmeyer (Minneapolis: Fortress Press, 1995), pp. 32-33.

which can have no transcendent, universal, or absolute content. This means, too, that the widespread tendency in contemporary theology to favor praxis over theory is mistaken — for it has its root in just this tendency in postmodern thought (and in its Marxist precedent). Instead, theology needs to insist on the meaningfulness of action in a different way, as something running *parallel* to theory rather than as something underlying it. Elsewhere, I have argued on trinitarian grounds that truth and love are reciprocal values and that any hierarchical view of their relation needs to be resisted.[5] This is not the place to repeat lengthy arguments from elsewhere but simply to note that such a view is presupposed in everything that follows. Thus theory and praxis, to use the categories prevailing in recent theology, are reciprocally related, and they mutually interpenetrate: you cannot have one without the other, each being equally necessary to the whole.

Troeltsch and Weber

In what sense, then, might it be possible for one's work, one's practical activity in the world — whether in the home or in industry or in voluntary activity — to be seen as a response to God? Let us begin again with some rather different sources, Ernst Troeltsch (1865-1923) and Max Weber (1864-1920), and with their sociological and theological exploration of the value of work in Christian culture.

If it is surprising to find that the New Testament is relatively untroubled by the question of vocation in the modern sense, it is equally striking that a similar attitude prevails throughout the early Christian centuries. Ernst Troeltsch drew

5. Gary D. Badcock, *Light of Truth and Fire of Love* (Grand Rapids: Wm. B. Eerdmans Publishing Co., 1997).

attention to this in *The Social Teaching of the Christian Churches* (1912), pointing out that the reason for this lack of interest was that the early church viewed social distinction and the whole question of labor from the standpoint of its theology of the fall.[6] The early church believed that at the beginning, before sin entered the world, an original equality prevailed. At the same time, the means of sustenance were given naturally and freely by God. It was only after the fall that inequality entered the world — first the inequality of man and woman, according to Genesis 3:16, but with it all the diverse ranks within society. Oneness was held on (Platonic) philosophical grounds to be the ideal; the plurality of the orders within society therefore had to be seen as an aberration from the good Creator's ideal purpose. Whether social division was defined more in terms of punishment for sin or simply as the natural result of the greed and cruelty that entered the world with sin matters little. After the fall, labor became necessary for survival. It is part of the divine curse that humankind should work for its bread: "cursed is the ground because of you; in toil you shall eat of it all the days of your life; thorns and thistles it shall bring forth for you. . . . By the sweat of your face you shall eat bread until you return to the ground, for out of it you were taken; you are dust, and to dust you shall return" (Gen. 3:17-19). The early church was frequently inclined to take a spiritualizing approach to the early narratives of Genesis, but this is a point on which, it seems, relatively literal interpretation prevailed. Troeltsch summarizes: "An ethic which starts from the point of view of an original equality, and which holds that the differences that do exist are due to sin, and which at its best regards the division of labour as a Divine arrangement adapted to the needs of fallen

6. Ernst Troeltsch, *The Social Teaching of the Christian Churches,* trans. Olive Wyon, 2 vols. (London: George Allen & Unwin; New York: Macmillan, 1931), I, p. 121.

humanity, is inherently unable to see any value in 'callings' at all" (*Social Teaching*, I, p. 121).

A series of factors combined to heighten the sense of social distance between Christians and the secular world in the early Christian era. In the first place, there was the emphatic requirement laid upon members of the church to give up any unworthy or immoral occupation, particularly if it was tainted by association with idolatry, the cult of the emperor, or the pagan sacrificial system. A Christian was thus forbidden to hold public office, serve in the army, work in the arts or the theater, sell meat, or even teach school because of the pagan associations of these occupations. By the third century, the requirements began in places to soften somewhat, but the truth is that what seems to us to be a very extreme ethical rigorism was the norm rather than the exception throughout the ancient church. Second, the influence of the doctrine of salvation itself is a major factor to be considered. The normal Christian understanding of salvation, not only among the common people but at the highest theological level, presupposed that the world is ridden with evil spirits to which humans are in bondage and from which they require redemption; once freed by the purchase price of the blood of Christ, the believer must hold aloof from everything under the power of the evil one, the one whom Christ himself called "the prince of this world." The church's eschatological expectation also played a significant role in distancing the Christian from worldly pursuits, while sporadic official persecution clearly must also have left its mark upon Christian attitudes toward participation in civil society. In the view of the early church, in short, the world is ruined by sin, whereas the true home of the Christian is in heaven. With such a view, it was impossible for the church to develop a positive approach to human labor.

In the case of medieval Christianity, one expects to find that the final triumph of Christianity in Europe would have

23

entailed the development of a more positive, world-affirming kind of social thought in the medieval church. This is in fact the case, and it was a change that brought about a corresponding reassessment of the role of secular and sacred work. The leading idea that enabled medieval theorists to develop a more positive conception of work was that of society as an organism established by the will of God. The idea of the original equality before the fall was not abandoned, for it was inherited from sources in the patristic era that were considered normative, but the less pejorative assessment of the state of the world as God's creation, despite human sin, required the development of a more positive understanding of work as conforming to the will of God. The world could hardly be regarded as ruled by the devil if now it had become Christian; thus a transformation of attitude was clearly needed, and it naturally followed.

Troeltsch, who structures his discussion around the patristic, medieval, and Reformation periods, regards the medieval era as making a new departure from the patristic period on these grounds (I, pp. 201ff.). Ordinary employment, whether in the fields as a serf or in the court as a statesman, is by no means seen as something sacred *in itself* — on this point the view of the Scholastics and of the Fathers differs very little — but the subjection of such work to the authority of the church as God's appointed channel of grace on earth genuinely gave to it what can really be described as a new theological status and dignity. The point is that the organic idea assumes that secular society can work in harmony with the church as a sacred institution: the church becomes the "soul" of the whole organism rather than merely a chosen remnant within it, or an ark to which the elect flee for refuge from the coming wrath. But this implies that the social order itself can share in the theological status of the church as a divine instrument for the salvation of the world.

According to Troeltsch, however, there is a real weakness inherent in the medieval vision, a weakness deriving from the conflict between two opposing tendencies within its grand synthesis. The first is the "rational" tendency toward the good of the whole organism, which is ruled by the ideals of mutual love and social responsibility; the second is the "irrational" and "patriarchal" tendency toward blind submission to the divine will, which ordains conditions of inequality as a punishment for sin (I, pp. 296ff.). The problem is that the latter tendency serves as a barrier to the kind of progress that might otherwise arise from the first. Thus, while the ideal of charity might have led to a revolutionary campaign to improve the condition of the peasant, for example, the more pessimistic patriarchal ideal militated against it. The result was an overdue emphasis in medieval social thought on the virtues of individual patience and humility rather than on social progress.

With Protestantism, of course, we enter a very different and much-discussed world of thought, and arguably a world in which for the first time secular work is able to assume a genuinely sacred status as a vocation. There is an enormous body of literature on this subject, most of it sociological rather than theological in character, deriving from the famous book by the social theorist Max Weber, *The Protestant Ethic and the Spirit of Capitalism* (1904-5).[7] Weber's claim is that in Protestantism, and in particular in Calvinism, the consciousness of divine election and one's worldly success, including success in one's economic life, came to be intimately related. In Calvinism as Weber presents it, a cold and rigid predestinarian theology of grace was combined with a rigorist ethic through the characteristically Calvinist emphasis on the doctrine of sanctification. One is to seek the proof of one's salvation, of the heavenly calling, in the fruit it bears in daily living. This led in Calvinist piety to the development of a secular asceticism, in which the

7. Max Weber, *The Protestant Ethic and the Spirit of Capitalism*, trans. Talcott Parsons, 2nd ed. (London: Allen and Unwin, 1976).

struggle to attain the assurance of salvation led to the subjection of the self to the service of God. Denied expression in the characteristic forms of religious life found in the medieval era, Calvinist piety thus assumed a markedly *secular* character. Inheriting the Reformation claims of Martin Luther that any worldly service is a vocation when carried out in charity,[8] Calvinism tended in the direction of a disciplined and systematic this-worldly asceticism. According to Weber, it was just such an approach to life that made the rise of capitalism possible.

Weber's arguments have been much discussed and have been widely challenged on a number of fronts, but there is evidence to support his contention at least to this extent, that over time the capitalist economy and Calvinist religion made happy company. One sees a crucial move in this direction within Calvinism by the early seventeenth century, when the English Puritan John Preston wrote: "How shall I know God's will and what my portion is? . . . I answer, by the event. See in what estate and condition God hath set you: see what estate he hath given you, that is your portion."[9] The point is not that wealth is an end in itself, or that it is God's blessing as such, but rather that it is evidence of spiritual standing. A godly, disciplined life will bear concrete fruit in the world, so that spiritual progress will be measurable by economic progress: "The more diligent a man is in his calling, the more sincere and upright, the more doth God bless him and increase his riches." Wealth is seen as a purely secondary blessing, to be

---

8. The main study of Luther's doctrine of vocation is Gustav Wingren, *The Christian's Calling,* trans. Carl C. Rasmussen (Edinburgh: Oliver and Boyd, 1958). See also the account of Luther that follows in Chapter 3 below.

9. John Preston, *Sin's Overthrow: Or a Godly and Learned Treatise of Mortification* (London, 1641), p. 246, quoted in Robert Martin Krapp, "A Note on the Puritan 'Calling,'" *Review of Religion* 7 (1943): 242-51.

sure, and is not to be sought selfishly, but the message is nevertheless wholly unambiguous. Here we seem to have an early version of what is sometimes called the "gospel of success" in American evangelicalism.

It was in this historical context, according to Weber, that the distinctively *modern* concept of the calling was born. One of the major characteristics of capitalism is the notion of the moral obligation, or duty, that one has to some professional activity. It was, he argues, Calvinist piety more than any other single factor that created the psychological conditions for the development of this idea, for here a single-minded devotion to work as a vocation with full religious significance was openly proclaimed. Weber's insight is what underlies the well-known phrase, the "Protestant work ethic," which has established itself even in popular conception. It clearly influenced Troeltsch, who wrote only a few years later, and who took up Weber's claim from a more constructive theological angle.

Troeltsch's work is complex — he was not only a theologian but a sociologist and philosopher as well — but his fundamental theological concern was to reconcile the *absolute* claims of ethics with the *relative* facts of historical and social change. Two assumptions govern his work: (1) The laws of morality are, as the philosopher Immanuel Kant had argued, universal and necessary, and yet (2) historical study reveals the growth and change of moral consciousness over time and across cultures. These can best be unified, according to Troeltsch, through the belief that the moral law can truly realize itself only through persons in history, rather than in philosophical or theological value systems. In the case of Christianity, the fundamental moral law is the law of love, as taught by Christ and by Paul. According to Troeltsch, this is expressed in terms of a union of the deepest self with God, and in a "socialism" in which mutual separation and strife cease (II, pp. 1004-5). Such values are only ever imperfectly realized, and always in

27

history, but according to Troeltsch they find their most complete expression in the Protestant ethos. Only in Protestantism — which Troeltsch understands primarily in terms of his native Lutheranism — can the ethic of a universal Christian society be carried through consistently. The reason is that the tendency of Protestantism to accept the life of the world means that it overcomes the dichotomy between church and world which prevails in patristic theology and which is only partially transcended in medieval thought (II, pp. 511ff.).

Vocation in this context, for Troeltsch, finally comes to be liberated from patristic otherworldliness and from the restrictions of medieval ecclesiology to become part and parcel of the public sphere of life appointed by God. The attempt to ground religion in the Kantian ideal of the moral law, and the insistence on the fact that morality pertains to everyday life, makes the attempt to flee the world theologically suspect. The great strength of Protestantism, he argues, is that it is thus able to regard all life tasks as genuine vocations (II, pp. 473ff.). Since there is no dualism of the supernatural and the natural, there is no longer any dichotomy between the "natural" moral law within the lower sphere of life and the sphere of the church, which rises above the world as the mystical body of Christ. Rather, the church exists in and for the world and fully accepts it. This does not mean that it is unable to grasp the nature of the world as something fallen; in fact, there is frequently an overdue emphasis on this in Protestant theology. The point is rather that such renunciation of the world as is practiced in Protestant piety is found in self-denial *within* the ordinary affairs of life, rather than in renunciation of the world per se. Protestantism leads to "an asceticism which is in the world, yet not of it" (II, p. 474).

Troeltsch is in all important respects a liberal Protestant of the early twentieth century, differing from others mainly in his adaptation of early sociological ideas to the task of theology.

Everything else — from his grounding of religion in morality, to his commitment to historical method and his search for a theological core that can be found in various forms but finds its most perfect realization in the Protestant religion and even in liberal Protestantism — is typical of the liberal school. What is striking is that, despite the demise of classical liberal theology in the middle decades of this century, the liberal theology of vocation has persisted in much Protestant thought.

Work as Response to God

There seems little doubt that the general contours of the sketch of Christian culture provided by Troeltsch and Weber are accurate enough. Though not all the relevant ground is covered — for example, the emphasis placed upon manual labor in the medieval monasteries does not receive sympathetic treatment, nor is the genuine note of otherworldliness sounded by the Reformers properly heard — the broad movement sketched toward a more positive assessment of the religious significance of the secular is undoubtedly true to life. We may say, in fact, that without this movement no positive theological assessment of work would have been possible.

It is, however, also possible to approach the theology of vocation from a more strictly theological angle, relying less on historical reconstruction and sociological analysis and more on the structures of Christian theology itself. This is what the rest of this book will attempt to do. The problem, of course, is that vocation as such is not a major theological theme. It is not mentioned in the great creeds, for example, and, as we have seen, it does not feature prominently in Christian theology down to modern times. Systematic theological expositions of Christian vocation are difficult to find. My goal, therefore, will be to locate it in a wider theological context and to make a case for the centrality of the concept of vocation in terms of this context. Of pivotal importance here will be the idea of response: vocation, I shall argue, is best understood in terms of the human response to God, and its central themes as a function of this wider question.

There are many theologies, of course, in which the concept of the human response to God is not a significant theme. The difficulty lies in the suspicion of the heresy of Pelagianism that hangs over all such talk. Pelagianism, which derives its name from the Celtic monk Pelagius, is generally described as the theory that human beings are capable of obedience to God by their own moral will without the direct assistance of God's grace; classically, however, it also involved the view that moral perfection is both commanded by God and a human possibility. Pelagianism, one might say, is a theology of pure response, or even of a purely *human* response. I do not wish to delve into the complex development of Pelagianism and semi-Pelagianism in its many varieties within Western theology, or into the almost endless polemics of theologians such as Augustine and the Reformers against it. Suffice it to say that a theology of response does not need to be Pelagian; it need only be theology in which the reality of the *human* is taken seriously. The encounter with God that is at the center of theology happens only in human lives, in short, so that the dimensions of that encounter must be susceptible to theological exploration and elaboration.

In fact, any denial of a human response in theology does violence to the whole point of God's own saving work as understood in the Christian faith. The coming of the Son of God into the world and the gift of the Holy Spirit are intended to result in the reconciliation of human beings to God — and reconciliation in biblical terms means that we are no longer strangers or enemies but children and even friends. The great commandment to love God with heart, soul, mind, and strength with which we began ought alone to be sufficient evidence that the quality of the human response to God is a central concern of the teaching of Jesus. In what follows, the case for including the world of work within this love for God, and an understanding of the *sense* in which it can be so included, will be developed.

CHAPTER 3

Calling

Luther

Martin Luther is one of the pivotal figures in our treatment of the Christian doctrine of vocation. His name has already been mentioned briefly, but it is necessary to consider Luther's contribution in greater detail, both because of its historical significance and because of its abiding theological interest. His own views, furthermore, are only inadequately reflected in Troeltsch's and Weber's work. We shall discover that the great Reformer of the sixteenth century still has important things to say and that his theology is able to shed a great deal of light on our way.

Luther's fundamental contribution to the doctrine of vocation stems from his view of what he called the "spiritual estate." The famous incident of the posting of the Ninety-five Theses in the autumn of 1517 — famous as much for its romantic elaboration in subsequent centuries as for its original importance — had by 1520 led Luther to the conviction that an axe had to be taken to the root of the medieval ecclesiastical system. One of the most important arguments used against that system appears in the treatise written that same year, *To the Christian Nobility of the German Nation Concerning the Reform of the Christian Estate.* "The time for silence is past," he says right at the beginning; "the time to speak has come."[1] Three "walls," Luther maintains, have been erected by the papacy in order to protect itself against the legitimate demands of the people. The first is the declaration that the spiritual power is above the temporal; the second, that the pope alone may interpret the Scriptures; and the third, that only the pope may summon a council. The first of these "walls" is the most significant, as Luther's treatment of it actually underlies his argument against the other two. It is also of great importance for us, for it is here that Luther's argument against the distinction between the spiritual estate and the temporal estate is most powerfully stated.

The theological distinction between clergy and laity and the social separation it implies between the spiritual and temporal classes was basic to the medieval outlook. Its origins lay both in early Christian asceticism, for which the renunciation of the world and the body was virtually required for a developed spiritual life, and in the increasingly hierarchical, sacerdotal view of the church that emerged in the early Christian centuries. As the church came to be seen as vested with spiritual power, and as this spiritual power came to be seen as concentrated in the hands of those chosen for ecclesiastical office or of those who distinguished themselves in the spiritual athleticism of monastic life, the clear distinction between spiritual and temporal estates was codified. The two cases of virginity and the priesthood crystalize the point. Virginity had come to

1. Martin Luther, *To the Christian Nobility of the German Nation Concerning the Reform of the Christian Estate,* trans. Charles M. Jacobs and James Atkinson, in *Luther's Works,* ed. Jaroslav Pelikan and Helmut T. Lehmann, 55 vols. (Philadelphia: Fortress Press, 1955-), vol. 44 (1966), p. 123.

be exalted above marriage almost universally by the fifth century; an enraged St. Jerome, for example, wrote a treatise *Against Vigilantius* in a single night in order to defend his own veneration of celibacy against criticism. The view of marriage as an inferior state prevailed in medieval spirituality and in theology, despite the general definition of marriage as a sacrament. A doctrine of priesthood also developed in medieval theology in which the sacrament of ordination rendered the priest qualitatively different from ordinary Christians: an "indelible character" imprinted on the soul placed him in a new relationship with Christ, a relationship that differed qualitatively from the one opened up in baptism.

Luther responds to the second of these ideas in *To the Christian Nobility* with what would become a leading theme of the Protestant Reformation: "we are all consecrated priests through baptism. . . . The consecration by pope or bishop would never make a priest, and if we had no higher consecration . . . no one could say mass or preach a sermon or give absolution" (p. 127). Luther's well-known argument is that there is only one status among those who believe, the status of being "in Christ" by virtue of baptism. Beyond this, any distinction between Christians is mere human invention, or at best something that exists only for the sake of good order. There is a common priesthood of all believers, for all are incorporated into the one great High Priest. Since it is faith in the gospel that makes us spiritual, the medieval distinction must be rejected:

> there is no true, basic difference between laymen and priests, princes and bishops, between religious and secular, except for the sake of office and work, but not for the sake of status. They are all of the spiritual estate, all are truly priests, bishops, and popes. But they do not all have the same work to do. (p. 129)

34

This is a pivotal point in Luther's thought. Following this, his early theology of ordination came to be worked out in terms of the common priesthood into which all are initiated at baptism; one is not selected by God from among the people to become one of the "chosen" ones, a "cleric" standing in some special relationship to God. Rather, the congregation delegates the responsibilities of its common priesthood to someone who has the gifts requisite to fulfilling it best: "It is like ten brothers, all king's sons and equal heirs, choosing one of themselves to rule the inheritance in the interests of all" (p. 128).

The question of virginity and marriage is also a central theme in Luther's theology. In the treatise *To the Christian Nobility,* Luther treats this theme summarily in connection with ministry: priests should be free to marry. Elsewhere, however, it is treated at greater length. Luther's denial of the distinction between the spiritual and the temporal estate, and of any superiority of celibacy over married life, is his main concern in all such discussions. In fact, the situation with celibacy is the reverse of what its supporters contend: because so many of those who take vows of celibacy believe that in so doing they acquire merit for salvation, and because they believe it necessary to the spiritual estate, they end by deceiving themselves and fall headlong to destruction. Such works can never take the place of faith; faith alone leads heavenward, it alone leads to eternal life, whereas the flesh profits nothing. Furthermore, there is no distinction between religious and secular works, as if God were more pleased with one than with the other. As Luther pointed out repeatedly in his 1520 *Treatise on Good Works,* to faith all works are equal, the reason being that they are acceptable to God only because of faith, which always has the same content in the gospel.

Another important aspect of Luther's estimate of marriage appears in a third 1520 work, *On the Babylonian Captivity of the Church.* This is one of the most important of all Luther's early writings, for it is a theological rather than a popular work, an attack on the medieval sacramental system intended for circulation among the clergy. Marriage, of course, was deemed a sacrament throughout the Middle Ages, largely on the strength of Ephesians 5:32, and is accordingly taken up by Luther. In 1519, before his excommunication, Luther himself had preached on marriage as a sacrament,[2] but now he rejects the sacramental view, arguing that whereas it is essential to any sacrament that it be a sign of a divine promise of grace, there is no biblical warrant for regarding marriage as a sign of anything. It had become, for Luther, purely a natural blessing.[3]

There is in Luther's thought, however, a close connection between such natural blessings, together with the responsibilities they carry with them, and the concept of vocation. One of the key terms in Luther's theology at this point is that of "standing" or "office" (*"Stand"* in German), which refers to one's station in life — the position in which one is set by God's providence. By means of these standings or offices of life and society, God's loving purposes in creation are fulfilled. Through the work of the milkmaid, God sees to it that the child is fed, that cheese can be made, and so on. Through the work of the ruler, God's just law is upheld and wickedness punished. Human labor and human agency generally are needed for the purposes of God to be carried out in the world; roast chickens do not fly spontaneously into our mouths, but are prepared for us by farmers and cooks. Thus married life, too, is a *Stand,* together with all worthy human offices and occupations.

All people have a standing, an office in the world. Every-

---

2. Martin Luther, *A Sermon on the Estate of Marriage,* trans. James Atkinson, in *Works,* vol. 44 (1966), pp. 7-14.

3. Martin Luther, *The Babylonian Captivity of the Church,* trans. A. T. W. Steinhäuser, revised by Frederick C. Ahrens and Abdel Ross Wentz, in *Works,* vol. 36 (1959), pp. 92ff.

one is a son or a daughter, a husband or a wife, a friend, a baker, a teacher, and so on. One does not, in fact, need to search far to see what one's responsibilities are or what one's standing is. Gustav Wingren, in his detailed study of Luther's doctrine of vocation, notes that this is the real basis of Luther's concept of Christian vocation.[4] The key is that vocation is a theological word, which applies only to the believer; the unbeliever has an earthly office but does not embrace it in faith as a calling.

As might have been expected, therefore, faith is crucial. Faith alone allows us to accept our worldly work as something religiously significant. Faith is also, however, what prevents us from seeing our worldly work as something that merits salvation. It is unbelief that leads one to search for works by which to influence God; by faith, however, the Christian can do what needs to be done gladly and willingly, without consciousness of reward, but solely out of a sense of love for God and in obedience to his commands. Faith lays hold of worldly tasks as given by God and pleasing to God, while also keeping us from the false presumption that by them we can be saved. Wingren cites a christological analogy from Luther's *Larger Commentary on Galatians* in order to explain this. Faith, Luther says, is separate from works, and yet it is poured out in works, just as Christ's divinity is separate from his humanity, yet poured out in it (*The Christian's Calling*, p. 41). Without Christ's divinity, his humanity would be nothing; similarly, without faith, our works are of no significance, except perhaps as the "works of the law," which can only lead to condemnation.

Luther's theology of vocation is therefore inseparable from faith, for he sees a sense of vocation as impossible without it. But one of Luther's most basic concerns is also to establish that

4. Gustav Wingren, *The Christian's Calling,* trans. Carl C. Rasmussen (Edinburgh: Oliver and Boyd, 1958), p. 2.

vocation does not refer solely to an ecclesiastical calling, whether priestly or religious. His doctrine of vocation is, rather, thoroughly this-worldly in the sense that it is always bound up with ordinary life and ordinary concerns — with secular work or with family life as much as with service in the church.

Wingren has drawn particular attention to the significance of the neighbor in Luther's thought on vocation (pp. 65-72). Vocation is generally something ordinary and near to hand. One does not need to either travel to distant corners of the world or retreat into the inmost self to find it. One finds it in one's neighbor. Vocation, therefore, is quite simply a function of Christian love. One might therefore characterize the whole of Luther's theology at this point, in fact, as founded on the two great commandments in Jesus' teaching. The love of God is expressed chiefly in faith, the love of neighbor in one's vocation. Because we all exist in relationship, in short, we all have a neighbor who is given to us by God's hand. If we search somewhere far from our present neighbor for the work that God entrusts to us, then we will in effect disobey his commandment. The tailor finds a way to love his or her neighbor in clothes-making and in fair dealing, the father or mother in being a parent. In the light of faith, these are embraced as divine vocations, so that the responsibilities of secular life come to have explicitly religious significance.

Finally, Luther's theology also has a response to those inclined to suggest that a vocation must be more than this, something more than ordinary. Because vocation belongs to the "kingdom of law" — that is, because it is a function of divine commandment, whether according to the law of nature or the Word of Scripture, rather than a function of the gospel as the promise of Christ's righteousness — it serves an essential function in the spiritual life. Its very ordinariness, its inglorious quality, the trouble and toil that it inevitably involves, serves the role of assisting us to put the "old man of sin" to death.

Vocation, in short, is a cross; as Wingren points out, one *bears* it (pp. 23-37). Vocation compels us to work for the good of others in love, to be selfless for the sake of the neighbor for whom Christ died. It is something directed beyond the self to human need, which means that it requires us to submit all selfishness to death. According to Luther, vocation is thus part and parcel of the dying with Christ proclaimed in baptism — the dying which alone can lead us to stand empty-handed before God, and which opens us up to accept his promise of mercy. Were vocation something more, something glorious or heavenly in itself, then its true heavenly purpose would be lost from sight.

Providence and Vocation

Luther's doctrine of vocation is strongly attached to a particular view of the stations of life as appointed by God in his providential care for the world. In this respect it contrasts rather sharply with the biblical understanding of the call of God, which is fundamentally about the call to faith and eternal life and then derivatively about the call to the service of the gospel. Only in one place does the New Testament possibly come near to Luther's understanding, the text already cited from 1 Corinthians 7. This text is fundamental to the Lutheran theology of vocation; but, as we have seen, it is questionable whether we can interpret it as Luther does. If his position is sustainable, it will in any case have to find support from more than a single proof text. Wider questions concerning the doctrines of creation and providence must therefore be addressed.

It must be said at the outset that there is much support in the New Testament for the idea that God in his creative power has established the existing orders of the world, and indeed that he watches over each intimate detail of its life. The

39

supreme examples come from the teaching of Jesus: "Are not two sparrows sold for a penny? Yet not one of them will fall to the ground apart from your Father. And even the hairs of your head are all counted" (Matt. 10:29-30). But the same theme can be found elsewhere in different forms — as, for instance, in the celebrated teaching of Paul in the Epistle to the Romans to the effect that political power, of whatever sort, is appointed by God: "there is no authority except from God, and those authorities that exist have been instituted by God" (Rom. 13:1). This argument, however, is clearly open to abuse. It was used by Christian thinkers for two millennia, for example, to justify slavery, and in more recent times it was allied with the theology of apartheid in South Africa. Closer to home, the idea of "station" also underlies the theology of woman's subjection to man — another idea whose time, we may say thankfully, is at length coming to an end. Thus the teaching is deeply ambiguous: if the sparrow does not fall to the ground "without the Father," does this mean that its destruction and that of its cousins through pesticides has occurred similarly? Or again, does the fact that all authority is appointed by God mean that the struggle against political tyranny really is (as Paul teaches) rebellion against God? Modern society has long since abandoned such ideas of providence, and Christian theology has generally followed suit.

If, in relation to the whole question of vocation, the original Lutheran idea of the "station" can no longer seriously be entertained, can the Lutheran doctrine of vocation still stand? In its original usage, the station is fundamentally a medieval and feudal conception, presupposing the idea of the social organism in which each member has a given part to play. The modern social ideal differs sharply, based as it is on the ideal of freedom. This gives rise, not to the idea of the life station, but to something very different: the goal of social mobility. This social mobility, I shall argue, raises entirely new questions for the doctrine of vocation and explains its peculiarly contemporary character. The universality of educational provision in modern times, for example, creates human possibilities that have simply never existed before. It is, of course, possible to overemphasize the extent of social mobility in the contemporary world, especially among the acutely disadvantaged, but for the majority of young people in every Western economy today, potential choices in life have been immensely widened beyond what they were even one or at the most two generations ago.

My own family history illustrates this. My parents were both born in rural Newfoundland in the second decade of the twentieth century. They received only a primary education, which was at the time in that society the norm rather than the exception. They were expected to do work in the fishing industry, in agriculture, and on the domestic scene throughout childhood and were withdrawn from school at a relatively early age in order to supplement the family income. The Great Depression of the 1930s only restricted further the limited possibilities open to them in their time and place. Their children, however, born amid the postwar boom in the Canadian economy, all benefited from a tertiary education and entered adulthood with a vastly increased range of possibilities open before them. It was thus that I, for example, the son of a poorly educated fisherman and carpenter (what theological precedent!) was able to become a scholar and writer. It is a familiar story, and one that could be told of countless millions of children in developed economies in the twentieth century.

What is often not appreciated by writers on the theology of vocation is that this new social situation also differs markedly from that of people in biblical times. The New Testament, for example, not only *does* not consider the question of vocation in terms of "career choice," but it *could* not have done so, for such a question would have been virtually unintelligible to its original audience. While it is true that in the ancient world the question of what *genus vitae* a youth should follow was discussed — as, for example, by the Roman writer Cicero in *De officiis* — it has to be said that, on the whole, there was never any real choice in the matter for the vast majority of humanity. Such has been the human lot for all but the most recent times in human history. When, therefore, Paul writes that "each one of you should remain in the condition in which you were called" (1 Cor. 7:20), he is making something more than a theological point about the immanence of the end of the world. He is also giving voice to his profound social conservatism, a conservatism that many today find shocking or even offensive: "Slaves, obey your earthly masters in everything" (Col. 3:22) and "Wives, be subject to your husbands as you are to the Lord" (Eph. 5:22) are two more obvious examples from the Pauline corpus.

It is difficult to reconstruct the life of, say, a pious Judean peasant farmer in the eighth century BC or that of a Christian cobbler in first-century Antioch, but we may surmise that such decisions as were taken in their lives concerning occupation and lifestyle were relatively few and were taken within rather narrow limits. In all probability, their occupations were hereditary, or at best were given them by virtue of an apprenticeship secured by parents. Thus, more than ecclesiastical tradition suggests that Jesus learned a carpenter's trade; the Bible may not say so, but as it was part and parcel of a son's lot in life to follow his father in the family firm, and as Joseph was a carpenter, this seems by far the most likely story. Certainly there was some social mobility in the ancient world. There were schools to which aspiring parents could send their sons if they had the resources; but there certainly was no universal provision, and for the most part the social strata of the ancient world simply perpetuated themselves by natural process.

For this reason, one cannot straightforwardly transfer biblical teaching concerning the call of God to the modern world. It is true that in the Old Testament the young David is taken from his flocks by God in order eventually to be made king over the people of Israel, and that in the New Testament Matthew is transformed from tax collector to apostle by a single phrase of Christ, "Follow me" (Matt. 9:9). But these are unusual situations, and the roles to which David and Matthew are called are unique. There is no suggestion that the stories are intended to serve as paradigms for vocation in the general sense, as if each Israelite or each Christian believer were expected to receive a similar summons to his or her divinely appointed role in life. If, therefore, we are to find guidance from the Bible in the modern context, in which the question of work has assumed new religious significance, we need at the very least to supplement such texts with additional ones and to reflect more widely on the question of God's will for humankind.

In Luther's case, the question of social mobility certainly does arise, but not in the way characteristic of modern times. Luther was the son of a miner and therefore had roots among the common people. In fact, this was to be an important factor underlying his popular appeal — much of Luther's ability to communicate in the German language, for example, stems from it. His theological education was made possible because of his decision to enter the monastery as an Augustinian. Thus, the very medieval system against which he wrote in later years was the source of the training that made him capable of his work as a Reformer. Despite this debt to the medieval system, Luther does not see his monastic vows in terms of a calling, though he is aware of the fact that it was through his life story that God set him in the church as a Reformer, nor does he universalize his own experience to make it the paradigm for the vocation of all. Luther wants universal educational provision, for girls as well as boys, but his objective is not to make social progress possible; rather, it is to raise the general level of literacy so that ordinary people can better understand the Bible. This ideal is also in accord with the new values of the Renaissance, for which the book and literacy were all-important. Luther even wants the peasant to have the pleasure of learning Latin, but he does not foresee that this might lead to the peasant being a peasant no more, or that it should have that effect. This would conflict, in fact, with his whole notion of the station in which God sets men and women by his providence.

It would be very strange to modern ears to hear Luther preach on the religious duty of the calling as rooted in one's standing. His whole conception of vocation as a religious duty is totally foreign to modern culture. Our notion of vocation invokes the virtues of choice, of freedom, of making one's own way in the world — in response to God, admittedly, but the response is nevertheless one's own. Luther himself would no doubt find our ideals strange and even judge them to be irreligious, a version of "works righteousness" and a kind of rebellion against divine order. At this point, a great gulf yawns between Luther's conception and the values of the contemporary world — so much so that it is difficult to sympathize with the prevailing tendency to view Luther as the prophet of the modern doctrine of vocation. There is a relation, undoubtedly, but much too much time has passed for us to make any easy transition from the Lutheran view to the contemporary situation.

The Ethic of the Kingdom

The goal of conforming to the will of God does not, as is sometimes said by the critics of religion, result in the abdication of moral responsibility. This is one of the most prominent criticisms of religion in modern times, the view that it involves a loss of self in the fiction of the divine will. According to

Marxism, for example, religious faith enforces a self-destructive social and moral inertia: the status quo becomes synonymous with the will of God, so that any genuine attempt to overcome forces of economic exploitation in order to govern excesses of wealth and poverty by human ideals becomes impossible. This theme is more than the invention of antireligious polemic. It features prominently in the theology of vocation itself whenever human work is seen in terms of providential spheres of life, and whenever society is conceived as an organism within which the various orders are set by God. Such a view of life was until recent times drilled into children in the well-known hymn "All Things Bright and Beautiful":

> The rich man in his castle;
> The poor man at his gate;
> He made them high and lowly,
> And ordered their estate.

Modern sensibility dictates that this stanza be deleted from our hymnals, though whether the total thought of the hymn is complete without it is an open question: Is nature ordered by God, and society not?

There is a real issue here concerning what the will of God is. But in principle, I wish to argue, conforming to the will of God is not an act of self-betrayal but an act of relating and submitting to the universally good. Because God is good, his commandments are good also: "the ordinances of the LORD are true and righteous altogether. More to be desired are they than gold" (Ps. 19:9-10). From the standpoint of religious faith, the capacity to seek to follow the will of God is so essential to the category of the human that there can be no question of an *abdication* of moral responsibility in serving God. It is, rather, the exercise of moral responsibility itself to "hear the word of God and do it" (Luke 8:21).

It is at this point that the distinctively religious aspect of the modern question of vocation arises. Where a person has no choice of career, or only a very narrow range of choices, since by virtue of social convention or economic and educational restriction the choice has in effect already been made, no moral question can arise — so long, at least, as the occupation is worthy. In the modern world, however, the possibility of choice is much more prevalent. For the middle classes in particular it is the norm. This introduces a new moral aspect into the whole field of work. To begin with, there is the terrifying responsibility of the decision itself, when the choice of one thing excludes other desirable options. Because the choice will affect one's life for years to come, as well as one's family and society, and because the route taken in life may genuinely affect one's own character, the whole question has an intrinsically ethical dimension. There is in addition a real possibility that the Christian, when faced with such a decision, *ought* to choose the occupation in which he or she can most effectively serve God. If one can choose, for example, between becoming a mercenary or an international aid worker, *ought* one not to choose the morally better way?

It was once the case, as we have seen, that the church proscribed certain occupations as alien to Christian worship and morality. This is usually still the case, though the number of occupations deemed immoral or irreligious has certainly declined. It would be perverse to suggest that a Christian could operate an occult bookshop or make a living by trading in pornography, and there is a clear case for ecclesiastical discipline when and where such things occur. Within the range of legitimate career choices, however, there is much diversity of opinion and a great deal of moral ambiguity. Does the company director serve the needs of the world in increasing the wealth of some at the expense of others? Does the legal professional do good by arguing the innocence of the thief? Or, on a different moral level, does the industrial farmer do what is morally right and serve God by relying on ecologically questionable agricultural practices? At such points, the church today often walks a tightrope between offering moral guidance and maintaining an emphasis on the moral conscience of the individual Christian; but it would, I think, be quite wrong for it actually to attempt to *proscribe* any such occupations.

It is, however, still possible to offer guidance to those making a choice of career; and for the Christian such guidance must surely derive from the ethic of Jesus, which is an ethic of the kingdom of God. According to the earliest of our gospels, Jesus' ministry began with the proclamation of this message: "The time is fulfilled, and the kingdom of God has come near; repent, and believe in the good news" (Mark 1:15). The kingdom of God is literally the starting point for Jesus — so much so that it is even possible to say that he defined himself in relation to it. Matthew tells us that the mission of the Twelve, whom Jesus sent out early in his ministry, was the same: "As you go, proclaim the good news, 'The kingdom of heaven has come near'" (Matt. 10:7). According to this text, the good news or the gospel itself is the message of the kingdom and its "nearness."

The kingdom of God is a notoriously difficult concept to interpret and has been much disputed in modern times. Interpretations range from the Kantian "kingdom of moral ends" in the liberal tradition through to a totally otherworldly, dreamlike expectation of the end of the world, as, for example, in the theologies of Albert Schweitzer and Rudolf Bultmann. For Schweitzer and Bultmann, all talk of the kingdom is purely mythological. This leads Schweitzer to a kind of theological resignation, and Bultmann to his own characteristic program of demythologization — the attempt to extract the religious or existential meaning from the clearly nonliteral, nonfactual sense of the text. One further interpretation of note is found in the theologies of Wolfhart Pannenberg and Jürgen Moltmann, according to whom the kingdom of God is implicitly about God himself: God *is* his kingdom, in the sense that God's being is his active rule.

It is not my intention here to pick what would necessarily be a tortuous path through the extensive body of literature surrounding this question. This would in any case amount to a treatment of much of modern theology, which has been preoccupied with it to a surprising extent. Nevertheless, I wish to state the case for what in theological circles has become a rather unfashionable view, which is that the kingdom of God is closely related to the question of human moral values, and that as such the idea of the kingdom has an immediate bearing on the doctrine of vocation.

Let me begin with one of the parables of Jesus, for it is surely the teaching of Jesus itself rather than the Jewish apocalyptic tradition that is the key source for the Christian doctrine of the kingdom of God. (In adopting this method, I might add, I part company with Bultmann, who adopts the reverse procedure and argues from the apocalyptic tradition to Jesus, thus prejudicing his conclusions from the outset.) The parable in question is that of the talents, told in Matthew 25 and in another form in Luke 19. The story is familiar. The owner of an estate went on a journey, entrusting his property to three servants: five talents to the first, two to the second, and one to the third. The first two servants put the money received to use while the master was away, and the money was multiplied. These servants were rewarded. The one who received the single talent, however, hid it in the ground; he took no risks, and though he handed back what he received when the owner returned, he did not meet the master's intentions in delegating responsibility for managing his estate. Upon the return of the master, the one talent was taken from the third servant and given to the first. The third servant (in the Matthean account) is thrown out of the household — "into the outer darkness, where there will be weeping and gnashing of teeth" (Matt. 25:30). The kingdom of heaven, Jesus tells his disciples, will be like this.

It is true that the context of the parable in Matthew, and to a lesser extent in Luke, is the theme of the apocalyptic return of the Son of Man to judge the world. The real emphasis of the parable, however, falls on the moral responsibility of those who do the work of God in the world. The world is likened to an estate in which workers are meant to set about their tasks. This, says Jesus, is what the kingdom of heaven is like. And as such it is, we must note, the kingdom of *heaven* — in other words, *that* kingdom is something having a direct bearing on life in *this* world. In Matthew, the same point is then immediately reinforced through what is sometimes called the parable of the sheep and the goats (Matt. 25:31-46), although the passage is not, strictly speaking, a parable at all. According to this text, in the last judgment all the nations will be gathered before the Son of Man in his glory, divided between the right hand and the left, "as a shepherd separates the sheep from the goats." The righteous will be rewarded for such things as feeding the hungry, clothing the naked, caring for the sick, and visiting the imprisoned: "Come, you that are blessed by my Father, inherit the kingdom prepared for you from the foundation of the world; for I was hungry and you gave me food. . . ." To the question, "Lord, when was it that we saw you hungry?" he will reply, "Truly I tell you, just as you did it to one of the least of these who are members of my family, you did it to me." The reverse applies to those who have not helped those in need; rather than entering eternal life, they will go away into punishment.

Such biblical texts are important, for they illustrate the strongly ethical content of Jesus' teaching regarding the kingdom — something also found elsewhere in the Gospels: "Blessed are the poor in spirit, for theirs is the kingdom of heaven" (Matt. 5:3). It is true that some teaching on the kingdom is more directly and obviously eschatological in character, such as the parable of the net in Matthew 13:47-50. But even here the purpose is not to give information about the end; rather, it is to urge repentance and moral reformation on the hearer: "The angels will come out and separate the evil from the righteous and throw them into the furnace of fire, where there will be weeping and gnashing of teeth." The point is not to be among the evil ones, not to be a "bad fish," of no use or value in the ultimate harvest.

One of the main preoccupations of scholars working in this area in the twentieth century has been whether the kingdom of God in Jesus' teaching is something that lies in the future or is something that can be said to be present now. The latter position is of special relevance for our theme, for although the connection between the kingdom of God and human ethics would be secure even if the kingdom in Jesus' teaching were consistently seen in futurist terms — for the final judgment is always in view in such eschatology — the connotations of the building of the kingdom in the present are even more important for the doctrine of vocation. Of all Christian theologians, it was Albrecht Ritschl (1822-1889) who developed this position most consistently, though perhaps not always convincingly, in the last century. Ritschl's is now an almost forgotten name, though his influence in his day was enormous, but his thought still survives in some popular theology. Ritschl saw humankind as called to establish the kingdom of God through love in the social and political arenas. It was his special adaptation of the Kantian philosophy, his Christ-centered approach, and the grounding of the whole in his detailed examinations of the history of Christian theology that made his theological vision such a profound and influential one in his day.

In the twentieth century, the name most associated with the idea that the kingdom is a present reality has been C. H.

Dodd (1884-1973), one of the greatest New Testament scholars of modern times. Dodd advocated a "realized eschatology," opposing the view that Jesus' teaching was futurist and apocalyptic (the so-called "consistent eschatology" associated with the name of Albert Schweitzer) with the idea that, for Jesus, the kingdom had *already* come with his own arrival. The sponsoring text for this version of the kingdom might be said to be Luke 17:20-21: "The kingdom of God is not coming with things that can be observed; nor will they say, 'Look, here it is!' or 'There it is!' For, in fact, the kingdom of God is within you." "Within you" is the marginal reading given by the New Revised Standard Version, the translators having chosen "among you" in the main text to translate the rather peculiar idiom of the Greek original. I tend to prefer "within you," but either translation supports Dodd's thesis. Dodd himself, of course, worked out his position in a series of books (*The Parables of the Kingdom* in 1935, *The Apostolic Preaching and Its Development* in 1936, and *History and the Gospel* in 1938), in which he examined the available evidence at length. His interpretation was certainly challenged, but from the 1930s his theology succeeded in placing realized eschatology firmly back on the theological agenda. Ritschlianism had been left behind, but the theme of the present kingdom returned to enliven Christian moral and political theology in Britain especially during the dark days of the 1940s and amid the growing optimism of the 1950s.

Today, however, with much of the heat of these theological battles behind us, it is more possible to take a moderate, mediating line on this question. Surely all attempts to interpret New Testament eschatology either in exclusively "consistent" or exclusively "realized" terms fall into the trap of insisting on an either/or solution, when the truth is that what is needed is a both/and approach. It is, after all, perfectly possible to allow for the presence of both futurist and present elements in Jesus' teaching, to resist the inevitable temptation to exclude inconvenient sayings from consideration, and to live with the resulting relative inconsistency. The merits of such an approach are clear, for once the aspect of the kingdom as something present has been secured, the present moral life of the believer assumes significance within it. The kingdom, for example, can be likened to a woman placing yeast in flour until the whole loaf is leavened (Luke 13:20-21). The yeast, it is clear, is Jesus himself, and his message; and yet his influence on the world being "leavened" is also part of his own work and part of the kingdom of God itself. Thus space is made in the gospel for the participation of men and women in Jesus' own mission, which is purposive, aimed at the regeneration of the world, and geared to fulfillment. It is in such a context that the Christian doctrine of vocation is ultimately located.

The values of the kingdom of God must thus inform and even determine the shape of Christian vocation. It is the kingdom of God that is to be sought before everything else, and not physical needs such as food and drink and clothing; it is those outside the kingdom who strive for these things, Jesus tells us (Matt. 6:31-33). The kingdom of God is a place in which little children are great; in it, the unimportant folk become important (Mark 10:13-16). What is prized in the kingdom is service rather than power (Mark 10:42-45). Where, therefore, the choice of career becomes a moral choice — where, in other words, the option to follow such paths is open to us, there the values of the kingdom must be allowed to inform the choice made. For this is part and parcel of what it is to be a disciple of Jesus Christ.

CHAPTER 4

Identity

The kingdom of heaven does not rest on the ruins of creation. In the same way, an adequate doctrine of vocation will never be built upon the rejection of human moral ideals. A vocation is something lived, something enacted in a concrete life story. Its primary reference is to the person called rather than to the God who calls: "What will I do with my life?" is vocation's question. God does not act out the details of my living for me, or even in me; instead, my existence is one of created freedom. Even though my entire being is dependent on God, I nevertheless choose and act, and I build my own life story through the decisions and projects that I undertake. On this view, a vocation is related to one's self-worth, and even one's worth for others. It is something built up through years of self-discipline, self-giving, and endeavor. It is not, however, universally accepted that such an approach is either necessary or possible in Christian theology. We turn first, therefore, to the foremost critic of this view.

Vocation in the Theology of Karl Barth

According to the great Swiss-German theologian Karl Barth (1886-1968), the fundamental content of the doctrine of vocation is really God's saving act in Jesus Christ, and not the particular story of the man or woman who is "called." In his theology of vocation Barth attempts to conform his thinking to the biblical conception, in which the whole concept of the calling is oriented to the call to faith and to discipleship, rather than to one's occupation or mode of life. The thesis that stands at the beginning of all that Barth has to say on this question reads as follows:

> The Word of the living Jesus Christ is the creative call by which He awakens man to an active knowledge of the truth and thus receives him into the new standing of the Christian, namely, into a particular friendship with Himself, thrusting him as His afflicted but well-equipped witness into the service of His prophetic work.[1]

The point throughout is to emphasize the objective ground and content of the gospel of God's revelation in Jesus Christ, rather than its subjective reception by the believer — even when the latter is really what is in question. The problem with this is that it fails to give human beings as God's creatures and as objects of divine love their due: in effect, they are denied any real status in themselves in the Barthian system of thought. This, as has often been pointed out, is one of the basic weaknesses in Barthianism as a whole, but its appearance in the context of the treatment of vocation is especially significant.

1. Karl Barth, *Church Dogmatics,* ed. T. F. Torrance and G. W. Bromiley, trans. G. W. Bromiley (Edinburgh: T. & T. Clark Ltd, 1962), IV/3, Part II, p. 481.

Barth's doctrine of vocation appeared toward the end of his life in the final completed installment of his massive *Church Dogmatics,* where it is treated in terms of his general emphasis on revelation as the central formal category of theology and in terms of Jesus Christ as its central content (IV/3, II, pp. 481ff.). In Jesus Christ, the Word made flesh, God is for humanity and humanity is for God: justification and sanctification have taken place, as Barth sees things, *in him.* But this "what," as he puts it, must also be realized by men and women in their temporal existence, which raises the question of the "how": How is it that we become hearers of the Word — indeed, doers of the Word as well? The answer, which will be familiar to anyone conversant with Barthian theology, is that it happens by way of a pure miracle, for this is the work of the Holy Spirit. Through the miracle of faith, the holy God claims for his own the unbelieving and sinful creature. Vocation has its place in this latter context, for Barth, and so is seen as a function of the question of the awakening of faith.

Barth's position can also be seen as representing something of a return to a classical Reformed doctrine of vocation, and it is actually more faithful to the intentions of that tradition than the interpretations of Weber and Troeltsch. It is true that John Calvin explicitly spoke in his theology of the particular duties assigned by God to each as "vocations" intended to regulate human life and to promote harmony.[2] To this extent, he followed the Lutheran tradition. However, one needs to be very clear that this is a decidedly minor theme in Calvin's thought and that it has to be set against his more characteristic emphasis on the general call of God to repentance and salvation and the specific call of some to ecclesiastical office. Reformed orthodoxy would speak of a *vocatio universalis* and a *vocatio specialis*, both of which, however,

---

2. John Calvin, *Institutes of the Christian Religion,* ed. John T. McNeill, trans. Ford Lewis Battles (Philadelphia: Westminster Press, 1960), 3.10.6.

referred to a heavenly rather than an earthly call: universal vocation was the invitation given to all by the proofs of nature to worship the one God; special vocation was the effectual working of the Holy Spirit to draw some to faith and salvation.[3] Though the sense of "vocation" as an earthly calling would persist in some Reformed thought, especially in English Puritanism, the idea of vocation as the heavenly call is found everywhere as the fundamental context within which all earthly callings are located.

In Barth's case, there is no question of a *vocatio universalis* in the classical sense; Barth is always opposed to the natural theology implicit in this, root and branch. In Barth, vocation is always tied to revelation, and revelation in a very real sense has its total content in Jesus Christ. Within these limits, however, Barth develops a twofold doctrine of vocation. It can, for example, be a synonym for conversion as the call to faith and new life that is met by obedience (pp. 497ff.). His more characteristic approach, however, is to speak of vocation in terms of the responsibility of being a witness. Barth examines the call stories of Scripture and concludes that their controlling principle is not merely that those called are set in a new relationship with God, but that the new relationship with God to which they are called always includes a commissioning and sending (p. 592). The primary model of vocation thus becomes the lives of the biblical prophets and apostles; like them, the Christian lives as a witness to what he or she has seen and heard. The point of this is that the Christian is made to participate, though obviously at a secondary and derivative level, in the event of revelation, as the revelation itself calls its own witnesses into existence. Vocation is thus located decisively within the structures of faith as a miracle of grace, and it is set firmly within the life of the church as a witnessing community.

3. Heinrich Heppe, *Reformed Dogmatics,* trans. G. T. Thomson (London: Allen & Unwin, 1950), pp. 510-11.

Barth, however, always refuses to treat humanity in itself as a subject of interest. His theology of vocation is the same: the argument is that the unique person and work of Jesus Christ are actually what is in question in the doctrine of vocation, for the divine call is to faith and obedience to *this* one and to no other. There is no suggestion that any sense of self-fulfillment or self-realization can legitimately enter into the discussion or that a free human response to God is what is in question. Rather, throughout the treatment of vocation, Barth focuses on the objective event by which humanity is set in the light of life. He argues that it is solely on the basis of the coexistence of Jesus Christ with us — on the basis of his existence as the God-man and his work as the Reconciler — that we have new life. But it is precisely this which constitutes the Christian calling, for it is the call to this new life and to its proclamation (p. 491).

Barth's intention in all of this is totally consistent with his whole theological project, which is to rescue Christian theology from the overt and overbearing concentration on the human that characterized the theological tradition in which he himself had been educated. Liberal Protestantism is therefore the great enemy. But with it, Barth also condemns any theological orientation or system that is focused, as he sees it, on the human approach to God rather than on God's act in Jesus Christ. The Catholic tradition of natural theology by way of the *analogia entis,* the "analogy of being," is also rejected, together with the very different "existentialist" approach characteristic of Barth's early collaborator, Rudolf Bultmann. The theological tendency he opposes thus has a long history:

> we usually describe a theology which looks in this direction as anthropocentric (though christianocentric would be a more exact definition), and we rightly regard Schleiermacher as its classical exponent, though we must also point to its

beginnings in the Pietism and Rationalism of the 18th century and even in the spiritual movements of the Reformation and the great mystics of the Middle Ages, and also to its unmistakable development in the modern theological existentialism influenced by Kierkegaard. (p. 498)

Against Barth, we may say that it is virtually self-evident that such a summary dismissal of vast and complex movements in the history of theology is far too crude. Nevertheless, the positive point is significant enough: for Barth, it is not the awakening of faith that is the central concern, but its objective content, the Word made flesh. Vocation thus becomes the event in which God encounters individual men and women in their concrete histories through his revelation, and therefore the event in which individual men and women in history encounter God and proclaim his Word.

Sharing Christ's Mission: Hans Urs von Balthasar

The most penetrating critique of Barth on this point comes from one of his greatest Catholic admirers, his younger contemporary and fellow Swiss-German Hans Urs von Balthasar (1905-1988). In his *Theo-Drama,* Balthasar constructs a case for the inclusion of human beings constructively in the mission of Christ and for the idea that the saving act of God is incomplete until it finds fulfillment in the life of humanity.[4] The point is that one never faces a stark choice between the Barthian theocentric approach governed by revelation and the opposing anthropocentric approach governed by some version of natural

---

4. Balthasar's writings are extensive, but the best single source for his theology is Hans Urs von Balthasar, *Theo-Drama,* trans. Graham Harrison, vol. III (San Francisco: Ignatius Press, 1992).

theology; rather, the whole story of the gospel is possible only through the interplay or interchange of divine and human freedom. His theology, therefore, recognizes the weakness of the Barthian system, which fails to recognize the fundamentally *humanizing* implications of God's loving outreach, and which correspondingly has no adequate theological anthropology. Balthasar's response is to insist on the role of both humanity and divinity in theology. This governs the structure and content of his theology from the beginning: both God and human beings have roles to play in the unfolding "drama." The act of God in Christ, therefore, is in itself an insufficient basis for the development of Christian theology. The sovereign Lord does not act in such a way as simply to subsume all human histories into his own incarnate story; rather, he makes a place for the whole human story in the salvation-historical drama precisely by entering the world of space and time. What is additionally needed in theology, on this view, is an adequate understanding of what it is to be "persons in Christ," which involves the positive role that we have in bringing the mission of Christ to completion. Humanity, therefore, has a genuine place in the kingdom of God. Balthasar's theology of vocation thus not only provides us with an incisive criticism of Barth but also represents an original and important contribution to Christian theology generally. As such, it merits extended consideration.

We may begin with one of the problems that has beset Christology in the twentieth century: the prevailing tendency to distinguish sharply between function and being in theological thought. The distinction is not one that I have ever personally found convincing, but the standard argument runs somewhat as follows. Biblical thought is concerned with divine action rather than with divine being. The latter is a characteristically Hellenistic construction, the former a characteristically Hebraic concern. Traditional Christian orthodoxy, which is mainly concerned with questions of Christology, has been developed predominantly along Hellenistic lines. The result is that, for classical orthodoxy, the being of Christ has been the fundamental question. This, however, conflicts sharply with the thought of the Old and New Testaments, for which questions of being (it is asserted) do not arise. Since it is developed along Hebraic lines, the christological faith of the New Testament is purely concerned with Christ's function, with what he did and with what he does in his continuing activity and influence. The rediscovery of the real character of the biblical witness, therefore, will lead to the rediscovery of the priority of *act* over *being* in christological thought and to the rehabilitation of functional Christology. In this context, it is Christ's function as Savior, and not his allegedly divine being as the second person of the divine Trinity, that is of real theological significance.

Such an approach to Christology has proven to be surprisingly influential throughout the twentieth century. It goes without saying, of course, that it has also had its critics — the most prominent of whom was probably Karl Barth, who insisted on the coinherence of act and being in his theology — but it has persisted in broadly the same form now for a rather long time. Balthasar, however, takes a different approach. For Balthasar, function is the key to being: there can be no question of beginning with a predefined "essence" either in the case of Christ or in the case of humanity, for human life is lived in freedom, which means that it is constituted by the acts and decisions made and taken in the course of life and time. According to Balthasar, God is also free (and here he follows Barth), so that one cannot define the divine being in advance, as it were, of God's own acts and decisions. This means that the concept of function, which encompasses concrete acts and decisions realized through action, takes a certain logical precedence over that of being in his theology, even with reference to God. It thus becomes possible, for example, to speak with the biblical writers of Christ *becoming* Messiah and Son of God. In this way, too, the whole of the encompassing framework of time and history within which the actions of God in Christ take place assume theological significance, for all acts take place in a situation and are related to that situation. Christ, therefore, is who he is in time, dynamically and relationally, rather than statically and timelessly.

Balthasar's position emerges through a consideration of two questions: first, the problem of Christology itself in the light of historical-critical biblical scholarship, and second, the concept of the person considered theologically. In the first place, Balthasar acknowledges that there is no ready-made path from the results of modern biblical research to the Christ of orthodox Christianity (*Theo-Drama*, III, pp. 101ff.). In the work of biblical scholars, Christ has frequently appeared in this century merely as an apocalyptic preacher of the end of the world. Balthasar notes the centrality of eschatology for biblical Christology, but he seeks to move on from a bare recognition of the importance of this theme to posit something of greater theological significance. On the face of things, the fact that Jesus lived within the horizon of eschatological expectation might seem to bear little or no relation to his messianic role. Balthasar, however, attempts a daring synthesis of exegesis and dogmatics at this very point: Jesus' consciousness of mission, he suggests, was tied up with eschatology, in the sense that he did indeed understand his mission eschatologically. That mission was nothing less than to abolish the world's estrangement from God in its entirety and to deal with the sin of the world as a whole (p. 110). Jesus' final "hour," which he both strains toward and dreads, was understood by Jesus himself as God's final judgment upon the old world of sin and the change to the new world of promise. That Jesus possessed such a consciousness of mission — a mission that was eschatological and universal — is something that Balthasar sees reflected in the New Testament. As such, however, the mission was unique, and so was the one who undertook it.

Balthasar presents his christological goal as follows: "a portrayal of the person of Christ that neither preempts the action undertaken by him nor falls back into [a] purely extrahistorical, static, 'essence' Christology" (p. 149). He cites in this context Oscar Cullmann's dictum that when the New Testament asks "Who is Christ?" the meaning is not "What is his nature?" but "What is his function?" The question of his *work,* Balthasar continues, implies the question of his *person.* Here the importance of the theology of the person emerges in Balthasar's thought. The question he poses is this: "Can he [Christ] be 'sent' in such an absolute sense that his mission coincides with his person, so that both together constitute God's exhaustive self-communication?" (p. 150). The answer, crucially, will be yes, for Balthasar will construct a case for the identity of mission and person in Christology and for an analogous doctrine of "theological personhood" founded on participation in the mission of Christ.

A number of convergent lines lead to this conclusion. First of all, there is biblical evidence to suggest that a new identity is given to people when they are given a mission, or given some preeminent mission. The paradigmatic cases cited by Balthasar are those in which men's names are changed: Abram-Abraham, Jacob-Israel, Simon-Peter. Identity is thus given along with mission. In Jesus' case, this is symbolized in the giving of his name by the angel. But it is fully realized only across time, in the totality of his life, as Jesus' whole existence is given over to the mission entrusted to him by his Father (p. 157). The general shape of Balthasar's Christology is thus consistent with this general thesis. He writes: "'Who he is' is exhaustively expressed in his being sent by the Father, who addresses him as 'My beloved Son' (Mt 3:17 par) — but the Son immediately recognizes this address as a call to be a 'servant'" (p. 172). To be the Son in time, in other words, is to have the peculiar mission of Jesus himself, the eschatological mission to drink the cup of God's wrath on the cross. His function in this sense is identical with his person. Balthasar summarizes his position as follows: "If we could put into words Jesus' fundamental intuition concerning his identity, it would be: '. . . I am the one through whom the kingdom of God must and will come'" (p. 166).

A further line of convergence is found in the notoriously difficult concept of the person itself (pp. 202ff.). Balthasar's discussion here is especially important, for the question of the person, he maintains, is fundamentally one of identity. I may know that I am a conscious subject, Balthasar argues, and that I am human in a unique way. But to know who I am is nevertheless extremely difficult. What is it that distinguishes me from everything and everyone else? Is it my physical location and qualities, my personal history and experience? If so, then I could, in principle, be a different person than I am now, for all of these are in fact accidents. No foundation can be constructed on such grounds for the concept of the person as possessing the unique dignity of humanity. A second possibility thus appears, based on intersubjectivity or sociality: I know myself only through the other, through the other's estimate of me. This idea appeared in modern times first in Hegel and subsequently passed in one form or another into many modern philosophical positions. The point is this: another values me, let us say a parent or a lover; I thus become aware of my own unique worth as indispensable to another's well-being or as the apple of his or her eye. But this, too, Balthasar rightly observes, does not yet secure the foundation needed. The best it can do is to tell us what I am *for the other person,* but not who I am *in myself.* "And as long as the conscious subject cannot discover his qualitative identity, he cannot find any absolute meaning, either, for his existence. . . . Everything is stuck in a web of relative, reciprocal, provisional values and revaluations, in which recognition is now accorded and now withdrawn" (p. 205).

The unspoken assumption, of course, is that such shifting sands are in fact intellectually and morally unacceptable and that some ultimate foundation for the absoluteness of human dignity is required. For Balthasar, such a presupposition requires no defense: it is self-evident. Without it, furthermore, the self is always in danger of being sacrificed for the sake of some pragmatic goal or other, some greater good. The guarantee of the person is provided, however, neither by the empirical world nor by the moral universe of our fellow men and women. "It can only be given by the absolute Subject, God. It is when God addresses a conscious subject, tells him who he is and what he means to the eternal God of truth and shows him the purpose of his existence — that is, imparts a distinctive and divinely-authorized mission — that we can say of a conscious subject that he is a 'person'" (p. 207).

The archetype of this is Jesus himself. In Jesus, the address of the Father constitutes his personal identity: "You are my beloved Son." Precisely because who he is is constituted by the address of God — because his personal identity is identical with his mission, in other words — he is nothing less than the revelation of the Father in time. "My food is to do the will of him who sent me and to complete his work," he says (John 4:34); or again, "Whoever does the will of God is my brother and sister and mother" (Mark 3:35). If it were not so, then the man Jesus would be someone other than the Son of God.

If the risk run in Balthasar's Christology is that the incarnation appears to derive from a rather "Nestorian" act of divine and human will, and that it may appear to some to fall short of a fully orthodox union of divine and human *nature* on such grounds — though this is a problem in much modern Christology — then one of its strengths is what it has to offer to a theology of vocation such as our own. For Balthasar has placed the concept of vocation at the center of the theological concept of the person, on both christological and anthropological grounds. The bare possession of a human nature, in his view, is something purely formal; it does not and cannot account for the distinctive and incommunicable personhood of Jesus, his personal identity as the one he was and is. So it is also with all human beings. The concept of the person is something unique, something particular and in a certain sense non-generic: there is only one of you or me. Balthasar's position is unashamedly theological at this point: without God, there could be no human person — not merely in the sense that it is the divine creative power and word which has brought human persons into existence, or in the sense that the human person is in some deep, mysterious sense the image of God, the absolute Person, but in the sense that it is the relationship to God as transcendent source and goal which calls forth from each individual his or her unique sense of selfhood. The relationship and the calling may be implicit; that is, it may be that only a sense of service to the good in the absolute sense awakens within the man or woman a sense of unique destiny or meaning. But ultimately, all such experience can be made thematic and explicit in the context of religious faith, and supremely (in Balthasar's view) in Christian faith. For in Christian faith, the character of the divine mission is fully revealed, and the nature and destiny of humanity are made plain. Human beings are destined to fellowship with God through the gift of God's own self-communication in Word and Spirit. As such, human beings are made the objects of divine love and care, to the extent of incarnation, cross, and resurrection — not to mention Pentecost and all its implications for existence in the church of God.

Balthasar insists that what most fully awakens a sense of the self as a person before God is participation in the mission of Christ, which has its goal in the realization of the kingdom of God (pp. 230ff.). The ultimate ground of this participation is christological: by the assumption of flesh, the eternal Son of God has assumed not merely a particular humanity but a relation to human nature in general. Human nature as a whole and as such is "the field of the mission of Jesus" (p. 231). Because of the sheer fact of incarnation, therefore, humanity — and thus, in principle, each individual human being as a member of the human race — is not only negatively redeemed but also positively endowed with mission. Such an incarnational approach to the doctrine of salvation is derived from patristic sources, as well as from the theology of Karl Barth, and represents one of the great strengths of Balthasar's theology as a whole. Balthasar draws at this point upon the classic theory of the "wondrous exchange" effected in the saving act of God in Christ: he became what we are in order that we might be made what he is. But the effectiveness of this exchange, Balthasar insists, depends not just upon the priority of divine action; it also depends upon the action of human subjects themselves in the freedom granted to them, as they awaken to the new personhood bestowed on them by the call of God.

A final point: one of the keys to a real understanding of Balthasar's theology is a proper appreciation of the significance of the cross. For the cross is central to his entire theology, and to his Christology in particular. Jesus, according to Balthasar, understands his mission as dealing eschatologically with the totality of human sin. The Johannine "Behold the Lamb of God" is something far from an anachronism, something placed on the lips of John the Baptist by the Fourth Evangelist several decades after the baptism of Jesus. It represents, rather, a summation of the whole character of Jesus, and even of his own self-understanding. To share his mission, therefore, must involve bearing the cross to which his mission was wholly oriented, and in which it was in a very real sense fulfilled.

Between Barth and Balthasar

The key differences between the theology of vocation in Barth and Balthasar are similar in many ways to the basic differences between the classical "Protestant" and "Catholic" approaches to the doctrine of justification. For Barth, the principle of *sola gratia* implies that sinful human beings can contribute nothing; their salvation and therefore the whole of the saving work of God, in the strict sense at least, rests upon something outside of them, something that happens in Jesus Christ as the mediator, and which is then secondarily imputed to them. This is the sense of justification by faith alone in Protestant theology: it is all of God, or more accurately, all of God in Christ. For Balthasar, on the other hand, there is a much stronger sense, deriving from the world of Catholic theological thought, that salvation involves a real change in the human being who is saved, a process of justification that is lifelong and that is essential to the saving work of God itself. One can speak of being justified by faith on this view, but not without love — so much so that the Catholic tradition can speak also of justification through love. The characteristic differences spill over into the two theologies of vocation, or into the different perspectives the two theologians develop on vocation. For Barth, the human element in the doctrine of vocation is at best a purely secondary implication of what is truly important; for Balthasar, the human is itself a basic constituent element of the whole.

There are clearly strengths and weaknesses on both sides. In the case of Barthian theology, the strength is the objective grounding of the concept of vocation in the act of God and in the will of God for humanity as revealed in Christ. There remains no searching about for a hidden divine plan; as T. F. Torrance has so often remarked concerning Barth, there is no God "hiding behind the back of God" who remains to be discovered. The true God has been revealed. Barthian theology also deals to a surprising extent with concrete political and social questions in order to outline the shape of the Christian response. Barth sees, for example, conscientious objection to the nuclear arms race and to unfettered capitalism as consistent with the Christian calling, and even as required by it. His theology has never existed in a religious ghetto, and it has certainly never thrived there. We need only witness the extent to which Barth's work was able to give inspiration to Christians resisting Nazism in Germany, and more recently to those involved in South Africa in the anti-apartheid struggle, to realize this. For Barth, such Christian social movements are parables of the kingdom of God, and as such they are part and parcel of the essential witness of the Christian to the gospel. There is thus much more to Barth than usually meets the eye at a superficial reading.

Nevertheless, there are major weaknesses in Barth's treatment of vocation, stemming from the problem that has already been highlighted: the lack of adequate attention to the structures of human life "in Christ." Barth's theology is anything but private and subjective, but in this lies its weakness as well as its strength: it is quite simply incapable of sustaining any kind of spiritual theology. This side of the question is much more fully developed in the theology of Balthasar, who discerns the importance of the human response to God as part of the fundamental structure of the gospel itself. For Balthasar, it is not enough to affirm in principle that because the proclamation of the gospel can take place only in the power of the Spirit, the response of faith on the part of the hearer of the Word is part of the event of revelation itself. This Barthian point is undoubtedly true, but it is much too abstract. It does not take into account the concrete reality of the human being or speak a language he or she can easily understand. The Christian is something far more than a hearer of the Word or a witness to it; rather, the Christian puts the Word into practice throughout the multivalent structures of his or her existence. The Word of God must percolate down through the self, to its depths, in order to be truly "heard" in the first place. This requires a sense of subtlety in theological anthropology that is entirely absent from the Barthian approach, and which it badly needs. It is much to Balthasar's credit that he attempts to provide it.

Neither Barth nor Balthasar, however, for all their differing emphasis on the doctrine of vocation, offers us much help concerning the extent to which it is possible to discern the vocation distinctive to each person. For Barth, vocation is primarily the call of God in Christ and secondarily the call to witness to God's revelation in Christ. How one is to carry out such witness actively in the world is left to one side. Similarly, Balthasar's doctrine of vocation as bearing the cross, and so sharing Christ's mission, may attempt to take adequate account of the constitution of the theological person through the Christian calling, but it does not answer the crucial question that most of us ask at this point, for in what sense each person is to do this is left as something of a mystery. Presumably, one discovers one's own way amid the rough-and-tumble of life, in the light of Christian faith and devotion. In his account of vocation, Balthasar simply assumes that such a thing is possible, and no doubt he assumes also that within the Catholic tradition the variety of spiritual paths that have been canonized over the ages and that have institutional expression in the various religious orders and the differing streams of theology within the church will help to guide the individual believer. But how this takes place is not discussed. Nevertheless, both positions travel some way toward the goal of discernment, in the sense that principles by which it might be possible to make particular choices in a life context are elaborated in the two theologies. How one moves from the universal principle to the particular situation or context, of course, is always the problem in moral theology, and here too the same problem arises. So perhaps the problem is one that, like the poor, will always be with us.

All the same, there is something distinctly odd about a theology such as Balthasar's, which attempts to argue the case for personal identity from a doctrine of vocation, but which seems unable to give adequate account of the way in which it might be possible for the individual to hear the voice of God calling and for the individual as such to respond. For identity is surely about more than what structures I may share with others: the fact that God addresses me as the object of his love is certainly important, but the question is surely also concerned with what is unique to me in my own situation. If it is my "theological personhood" before God that is at stake in the doctrine of vocation, then it is surely necessary to pose the question how it is possible for me to hear the voice of God speaking, not just in a general sense but to me, and to address the question explicitly of how it is possible to discern the will of God.

CHAPTER 5

The Source

God as Source

The source of vocation must be none other than and no less than God himself. Although a sense of vocation is intrinsically related to the objective facts of one's human capabilities — one's "gifts and graces" — the explanation for the real power of a vocation to rule the course of a life lies in the fact that it comes from God. My vocation is to this extent something laid upon me, an obligation that I must pursue: "woe to me if I do not preach the gospel!" Paul remarks at one point (1 Cor. 9:16). This is nothing unusual; in fact, a sense of obligation, or of service to some higher cause, is one of the prerequisites even for psychological well-being. Whatever the philosophers may say, we live in a world of universals and orient our lives toward them. The devoted father "lives," in a very real sense, for his family; the skilled craftsman derives satisfaction in a job well done — "beautiful and useful" is his ruling principle; the ward sister, underpaid and overworked, fulfills a moral duty in nursing the sick. The real question is what our own ruling principle is, and what the nature of such universals is.

71

Philosophically, of course, this is a major question — indeed, it is in a very real sense the *only* great philosophical question. For the Christian, however, the answer is clear: both the universals and our own ruling principle have their source and their root in God.

Properly speaking, of course, it is only when the task laid upon a person is taken to be something commanded by God that the question of a *calling* strictly arises. It is God, God alone who calls, for only God has the right to demand the unconditional obedience and sacrifice that make up the life lived in faithfulness to a calling. This explains the otherwise impenetrable demands of Jesus. Because God is making his appeal through him, Jesus is able to require a total surrender of the self to his cause: "those who want to save their life will lose it, and those who lose their life *for my sake* will find it" (Matt. 16:25, emphasis mine). "For my sake" means "for the sake of my mission, in keeping with it and to help to fulfill it"; it is because Jesus' cause is nothing less than the kingdom of God that he is able to call others to unconditional discipleship. And we may say with total confidence that it is only to the extent that people catch this vision that they can find themselves "called" in the Christian sense. For the Christian calling is not something vague or general; it does not stem from a nonspecific sense of the rhythm of nature or from unfettered exploration of the inner self. It stems instead from an encounter with the holy, with God, with the transcendent source of all human hopes and possibilities — and more specifically, from that source as encountered in Jesus Christ and in the church as his worshiping community. This is why a vocation is always to be understood in terms of bearing the cross: it is something we share with Christ in some small measure, a part of his mission in the world, something that requires a death to self for the sake of God and other people. It is not *primarily* about self-discovery or self-fulfillment at all, but about finding one's life by losing it for Christ's sake — that is to say, for the sake of his mission, for the sake of the kingdom of God.

The fact that God is the source of vocation has a number of important implications. It may be the case that some rare person is capable of holding onto the sense of divine presence and vocation throughout life. But it is much more reasonable to expect that such sense of vocation as we may have will be traceable to some core experience or insight along life's way, and not to a day-to-day experience. A vocation does not come fresh to us every morning, as if it were always something new, or as if God had either the need or the inclination to remind us of it regularly before breakfast. The source experience may even be far in the past and not something within present reach at all. This is a helpful thing to realize, for there are people who look for their calling in the wrong place. It may be that the most fruitful place to look will be in something experienced during some phase of the spiritual life some time ago. It is often a sensible policy to make life decisions based on what the psychologist Abraham Maslow has called "peak experiences"[1] and to avoid making such decisions during life's troughs. In many traditional human cultures, and certainly in biblical times, to do this has been understood in terms of following a "vision." It is important also to note, however, that the experience in question may actually be some experience of suffering, but suffering that has left a meaningful mark on the self, so that it thus becomes a source of positive development. Perhaps the term "depth experience" in this case would be preferable. The British charity The Samaritans, for example, was founded by a devastated young Anglican priest, Chad Varah, following the tragic suicide of a young parishioner, and it has subsequently helped many desperate people to talk out their

---

1. Abraham Maslow, *Religions, Values, and Peak-Experiences* (New York: Viking Press, 1970).

troubles.[2] One could never speak of the initial impetus as a good thing, but at least good came out of evil in this case.

In the Bible, the experience of God is often at one and the same time the experience of a calling, and so it is also today. But we cannot expect this to be repeated constantly. Nor can we expect a directly verbal commandment to be given — at least, not ordinarily. Saul may have heard the risen Lord speak to him on the road to Damascus, but most of us hear God's voice only through the reading or preaching of Saul's story, and those of others like him. And yet the voice of God is heard, for the source of all human good wants to make himself and his will known. The key is to let him speak as he will and not to look for him to say only what we want, when and where we choose. Wisdom, as the opening chapters of Proverbs teaches, is found by those who seek her, but only on her own terms.

The Role of the Bible

Acknowledgment must be made of the role of the Bible in mediating the voice of God, for this is the consistent witness of the people of God through the ages. At the end of his tether, Augustine, for example, sat looking for peace in a friend's garden in Milan and heard children's voices (for so it seemed) singing, "Pick up and read, pick up and read."[3] He took the voice to be a divine command, for there were no children nearby, looked about, and found an open Bible in the place. He then read the first passage his eyes fell upon, an ethical text

2. For an account of the Samaritans, see Chad Varah, ed., *The Samaritans,* rev. ed. (London: Constable, 1987).

3. St. Augustine, *Confessions,* trans. Henry Chadwick (Oxford: Oxford University Press, 1991), 8.12.29.

from the Epistle to the Romans: "not in reveling and drunken-
ness, not in debauchery and licentiousness, not in quarreling
and jealousy. Instead, put on the Lord Jesus Christ, and make
no provision for the flesh, to gratify its desires" (Rom. 13:13-
14). Augustine had been raised a Christian and had of late
heard the great Ambrose's preaching; yet it was this text encountered in such a situation that somehow broke the waters,
and from it flowed his conversion. He had, without doubt,
heard it before, but at last it went to his heart and transformed
him. The stories could be multiplied endlessly from all eras,
for there has never been a Christian who has not similarly been
"struck" by *something* of the contents of Scripture, which has
then served as food and strength for the journey of faith. The
vast majority of their stories are hidden, but the great paradigms
tell the tale as well as it can be told: God speaks through his
Word.

In order for this to take place, however, there must be a
bridge of some sort between the page and the situation of the
reader, an imaginative leap from Bible to life; for whatever
influence the Bible has upon us takes place in our own minds
and consciences. There is nothing intrinsic to the story of the
"rich young ruler," for example, to *compel* the kind of moral
and religious assent that has characterized some lives, but
compulsion of a very real sort there has been. If I might speak
on a personal level, there was nothing intrinsic to a set of texts
concerning "white raiment" found randomly in a Gideon's Bible
in a Canadian university dormitory to compel my assent and
lead to a transformation of my values. Yet one night the words
leapt off the page and made their home within me. No doubt
a psycho-social explanation is possible. Perhaps an insecurity
at the time prepared the way for such spiritual influence. But
it was an experience that I certainly could never re-create of
my own will, even were I capable of surmounting the odds
once more and of flipping open a Bible randomly to find my

eyes again set upon the few passages in the Old and New Testaments mentioning white garments, the symbol of righteousness. Even here, however, the imaginative bridge was an essential part of the influence that the Bible had upon me. The words had to be related to life and interpreted spiritually in order for them to have their effect: it is not the letter but the Spirit that gives life.

The spiritual interpretation of the Bible is one of the things we have to insist upon at this point — and one of the things contemporary theology needs most desperately to recover. Such interpretation was long standard in biblical exegesis, was criticized at the time of the Reformation (though in fact the Reformers and their successors continued to practice a version of it), and finally passed from the scholarly scene in the context of the Enlightenment, when the methods of modern historical-critical biblical scholarship were developed. In fact, of all the theological disciplines, biblical scholarship today is the most moribund: the same methods, arguments, and endless scratching at the surface of the text (the "letter" rather than the "Spirit") that characterized the methods of the Enlightenment scholars unfortunately still characterizes the work of many contemporary exegetes. There have been advances, and clearly attention to historical detail is necessary, but the text was never *intended* to be read this way. Origen, the greatest exegete and theologian of the Eastern Church, was much nearer the truth in the third century when he said that attention to the "literal sense" is the lowest form of interpretation; when exegesis rises no higher so as to serve the spiritual needs of human beings, it becomes a hindrance rather than a help to theology, and even the source of heresy.[4]

4. For an excellent account of Origen's exegetical methods, see Henri Crouzel, *Origen*, trans. A. S. Worrall (Edinburgh: T. & T. Clark, 1989), pp. 61ff.

It ought to be self-evident that without some such procedure of spiritual interpretation, however construed, there is little possibility of finding guidance in the Bible, of hearing God speak through it in such a way as to give religious direction to life. On such a view, the Bible might best be understood as a *sacrament:* something earthly that, by the mystery of God's presence, becomes at another level the bearer of God's grace. In its own intrinsic "substance," it is and remains just a book, a human document representing so many thousands of years of accretion, synthesis, and commentary. But the real meaning and power of a sacrament does not exist, strictly speaking, at the literal, physical, or historical level. Its meaning, rather, lies "above" it, in what it signifies rather than in the sign itself. What is important about the Bible lies not so much in the text as a historical artifact, or even as a religious-social construct, but "above" it. The Bible points beyond itself in such a way that its true function is to provide a series of approach roads to God. Or, putting this another way, the meaning lies "above" the text in the sense that it lies in the interpretation and application that take place on the nonliteral, spiritual level. This is why prayer is so important in approaching it, for such interpretation is possible only in the context of prayer, where a man or a woman opens up to God, speaks to God, and allows God himself to speak as well.

The Voice of God

The whole concept of divine "speech" in connection with the Bible and revelation generally is, however, a controversial subject. In fact, the idea that a person should hear the voice of God speaking seems very foreign to much contemporary Christianity. True, within charismatic circles the gifts of the Spirit are often associated with claims to explicit and even verbal supernatural direction. Among the list of *charismata* in 1 Corinthians 12 are to be found gifts of knowledge, prophecy, and discernment, along with the more familiar (and notorious!) gift of tongues. Each, however, involves forms of intelligible speech to some extent or other, and each is intended to result in what can only be described as inspired human discourse. The use of such charismatic gifts to give direction is one of the standard features of the charismatic movement. The claim is that the Holy Spirit of God is immediately experienced within the worship of the church, so that the notion of a direct commandment from God coming to people is not seen as at all impossible or even unusual. The model church, seen from the charismatic angle, is rather like the situation described in Acts 13:1-3, where Barnabas and Saul (later Paul) are sent out by the church at Antioch, following a prophetic word given in the context of prayer and fasting. But it would hardly do to speak of such experiences as typical within the Christian church as a whole today.

Even the alternative tradition within Protestantism, according to which the voice of God can be heard in the context of Bible reading, is widely challenged. The reasons for this, of course, vary widely. There is obviously the pervasive religious skepticism of modern culture to contend with, according to which God, if he exists at all, has no real relation to the world, and certainly not to the ordinary world of everyday affairs. It is a hard thing to expect the secularized men and women who for the most part people contemporary Western churches to step out of their cultural skins for ten minutes a day or on a Sunday morning in order to hear God "speak." We do not tend to think of hearing voices in one's head, or of seeing visions, with approval. Such experience nowadays leads as often as not to the psychiatrist's chair.

More than this, the theology of revelation that has predominated in twentieth-century theology — in particular in

Protestant circles — has tended to militate against the notion that God should in any sense speak directly to men and women. John McIntyre draws attention to this factor in the contemporary situation in a discussion of the theology of prayer.[5] Revelation in much theology has become, not the propositional communication of truth by God, or of his will, but rather the offer of the living God himself, the divine self-disclosure by which men and women are brought into contact with God. On this view, the primary revelation is Jesus Christ himself in person, rather than speech about him or any other propositional communication. McIntyre goes on to raise the question regarding what this means for our concept of prayer — for propositional speech moving in the Godward direction — a question too little examined by the proponents of this doctrine of revelation: "If we move away from propositional revelation, and if we construe the responsive moment in revelation on its human side in terms of obedience, acknowledgment and even 'faith,' then the role of old-fashioned, articulate speech in our relation to God has to be re-examined." He continues, "I would go so far as to suggest that here, in the heart of so much contemporary orthodoxy, is actually to be found one of the sources of . . . [the strange fact] . . . that some religious people believe in God and in revelation but are desisting from the practice of any traditional kind of prayer" (p. 176).

Over against such tendencies we need to set the clear biblical expectation that God can and does speak. Obviously, such biblical language can only be analogical: to say that God speaks surely does not mean that God literally has lips, tongue, and voice. McIntyre, who examines the biblical material at length, suggests that an analogy with some of the insights taught

5. John McIntyre, "Theology of Prayer," in *Theology After the Storm,* ed. Gary D. Badcock (Grand Rapids: Wm. B. Eerdmans Publishing Co., 1996), pp. 172-77, 195-212.

in basic philosophical epistemology is relevant at this point (pp. 190, 208). Objects in the world may appear to be colored, to have a taste, and so on, but philosophers have for the most part agreed that naive realism is impossible: the color and the taste are how the objects appear *to us,* not how they are in themselves. Similarly, McIntyre suggests, it is possible to understand the notion of propositional revelation as propositional *for us,* though not, presumably, for God. For if God is to communicate with creatures who use language to communicate, it is difficult even to imagine how else he might achieve his goal: "his communication must eventually be convertible into verbal, conceptual, propositional form. But we are not thereby affirming that the source of the communication is verbal, or even that God's response can be atomised into discrete thoughts" (p. 209).

There would seem, therefore, to be no intrinsic reason why God, wishing to communicate with humanity, should not do so in verbal form. His voice need not be physically audible; and in fact, in the Bible all claims to have literally heard the voice of God speaking occur in the context of some sort of visionary experience. What is encountered at this level is not, as it were, literal reality. And yet, the claim is never to have encountered God at the purely physical level; the whole complex of ideas is thus at least internally consistent. There is every reason, therefore, why someone who believes in a personal God who wants to make himself known to human beings should also believe that such a God is capable of "speaking," in the sense of making his message known in some verbal form.

This is hardly radical theology, but the point needs to be made, because the accusation of mythologization at this point is so prevalent and indeed pervasive on the contemporary theological scene. Such an approach is also necessary for an adequate theology of Scripture. It does not, however, commit us to any crudely literalist doctrine of verbal inspiration, nor does it imply that we must therefore interpret the Bible literally.

For one thing, as the church Fathers recognized long ago, the Bible leads to heresy when interpreted literally; "Our God is a consuming fire," says Hebrews 12:29, but this does not mean that God is a chemical reaction leading to the release of energy in hydrocarbons! The danger was perhaps more subtle when fire was considered one of the four mysterious physical elements making up the cosmos, but the theological response then and now must be the same. As to verbal inspiration, it is necessary to understand the Bible's message as mediated through history, character, and culture as much as through the direct act of God; the whole thrust of the idea of inspiration is that God lays hold of such finite creatures as people and language and uses them to his purpose. Inspiration, therefore, presupposes a *condescension* on God's part, and we have every reason to believe (given the cross in particular) that God's condescension in reaching out to the world is something total and even relentless in character. The idea of the Bible being dictated by the Holy Spirit in such a way that prophets and apostles merely wrote down what they heard — in Hebrew, Aramaic, and Greek no less — is not just something that critical biblical scholarship despises. It is also without wider theological foundation; for in his relations with us, God enters wholly into the ambiguities of the world he loves.

The Will of God

Does God have a tailor-made will for each individual? I have already suggested that this is not so. If it were, then each calling would have to be totally unique. Admittedly, some biblical teaching suggests that each occurrence in time is foreordained by God's providence, which might suggest that there is a unique plan for each human life as well. But the strong doctrine of foreordination is not the universal view of biblical writers, who also speak of sin as human rebellion against God's will. The doctrine of vocation that is rooted in providential "stations" laid down in intimate creative detail by God has also been challenged; it can shed light on the question, as we shall see, but it is also open to the gravest abuse. And although the call of the prophets differs from one case to the next, just as does the call of the Apostles — Peter to the Jews, Paul to the Gentiles — the fact is that the will of God as the Bible presents it is mainly general rather than specific; for on the whole, it relates to humanity in general rather than to particular individuals. It is expressed in such things as the divine law of the Old Testament and the ethical instructions of the New. To those who cast about looking for evidence of God's will in external facts or events, or within the inner self for guidance, the Old Testament prophet Micah has a ready answer: "He has told you, O mortal, what is good; and what does the LORD require of you but to do justice, and to love kindness, and to walk humbly with your God?" (Mic. 6:8). It is generally much more important to do this where we are than it is to seek some different role in the world.

Nevertheless, it does appear in the Bible that God does have a specific plan or purpose for some individuals. "Before I formed you in the womb, I knew you, and before you were born I consecrated you; I appointed you a prophet to the nations," he says to Jeremiah (Jer. 1:5). Paul says the same thing of his own ministry: "God . . . set me apart before I was born" (Gal. 1:15). But what is distinctive about such thinking is that it does not refer to everyone, any more than becoming a prophet or an apostle happens to everyone. The prophet or the apostle is unique; if this were not so, then everyone called by God would by that very fact be his or her own prophet. In the context of contemporary religion, this might actually be something of a temptation, for it resonates somehow with the deep-seated individualism of modern culture. But it is totally foreign to biblical thought, for which the passages cited are actually warrants for the authority *over us* of people such as Jeremiah and Paul, who act as the spokesmen of God. For the rest of us, and for all of us most of the time, the will of God as understood in the Bible consists in living faithfully and lovingly, being obedient to the commandments, and seeking "the things that are above" (Col. 3:1).

It is here that the special genius of Luther's position appears. The will of God, according to Luther, is close to home: one finds it simply in loving God and, crucially, in loving one's neighbor. As we have seen, the role of the neighbor is of special importance, for in the neighbor lies the rationale for Luther's language of secular "callings." In serving the needs of the person next to us, whether in the home with the child or husband or wife, in the shop or the fields, in the classroom or the court, one can do the will of God by doing good, by "doing justice" and "loving kindness." In a very real sense, this is all that is needful. The whole world, we might say, is full of moral significance, and in fulfilling our ordinary responsibilities to others we find and fulfill our calling. Any calling is unique to the extent that our own special situations, our relationships and the needs that arise in them, are unique. But in the strict sense, we find the will of God in our role within the whole of the social order established by God for the human good.

Luther's achievement here was to invest ordinary occupations with religious significance, with the dignity of a "calling." Nevertheless, we need to ask whether he allowed the distinctive emphasis of the biblical writers to shine through to a sufficient extent. For in the Bible, the call is generally to a sacred rather than a secular role, a role that is discontinuous with the ordinary social sphere, and even with natural human existence as such. To seek the things that are above, in short, means *not* to seek the things that are on earth. For this reason, we need to explore more fully the relation of sacred to secular in the theology of vocation.

CHAPTER 6

Sacred and Secular

The Heavenly Calling

There is little talk of heaven in modern theology. In fact, the whole concept of transcendence has become something foreign to our intellectual culture; our philosophy, our literature, and even much of our theology have been emptied of it. It is not just that the pervasive consumerism of our society betokens a fundamentally materialist understanding of life and set of values. Transcendence, rather, has actually become something theologically suspect. To "die and go to heaven" once constituted the goal of life in the popular understanding of the Christian doctrine of salvation, reflecting the otherworldly tendencies of traditional Christian thought. Today there is a great deal less confidence in such talk. Many theologians nowadays tend to speak instead of divine immanence and of salvation as liberation, and to emphasize themes such as the social context of theology. Theology is best "engaged," it is said, with the ordinary sphere of life; otherwise, it becomes detached, ideological, abstract, and ultimately unreal.

In the New Testament, however, things appear to be very

different. All the most important strata of the New Testament reflect a preoccupation with the heavenly that is truly basic to its outlook. "Do not store up for yourselves treasures on earth, where moth and rust consume and where thieves break in and steal; but store up for yourselves treasures in heaven, where neither moth nor rust consumes and where thieves do not break in and steal. For where your treasure is, there your heart will be also" (Matt. 6:19-21). We have often heard the words of Jesus, but it scarcely needs to be pointed out that we are not inclined to take them overly seriously. We still read up on our investment strategies and lay our plans for retirement, almost as if these were the goals of life. Jesus' words, however, suggest that this is ultimately futile.

A concern for the hope of heaven is not restricted to the synoptic Gospels. The Gospel of John teaches the same thing again, though in its own distinctive way: "In my Father's house are many rooms; if it were not so, I would have told you. I am going there to prepare a place for you" (John 14:2, NIV). It is true that Jesus also speaks of the earthly mission of his disciples in John — "As you have sent me into the world, so I have sent them into the world" (John 17:18) — and of his continuing presence with them through the Paraclete. Indeed, it would be fair to say that the basic thrust is *toward* the world rather than away from it in the Gospel as a whole. But this does not do away with the fact that the source of the initiative is the "Father who is in heaven" and that the ultimate goal is to be with Christ where he is now, risen, exalted, and ascended. At the end of the so-called "high-priestly prayer" of John 17, Jesus makes this clear: "Father, I desire that those also, whom you have given me, may be with me where I am, to see my glory, which you have given me because you loved me before the foundation of the world" (17:24).

It is Paul, however, who expresses the hope of heaven most fully and eloquently in his theology. One finds the theme in a variety of places. For example, the classic resurrection-of-the-dead text, 1 Corinthians 15, speaks of the transformation of the body from something "physical" to something "spiritual" (15:44ff.). Paul's interest in the postmortem state is also obvious in 2 Corinthians 5:1: "For we know that if the earthly tent we live in is destroyed, we have a building from God, a house not made with hands, eternal in the heavens." But the fundamental text must be the Epistle to the Philippians, where Paul speaks in intensely personal terms of how, "forgetting what lies behind and straining forward to what lies ahead, I press on towards the goal for the prize of the heavenly call of God in Christ Jesus" (Phil. 3:13-14). The "heavenly call" here can also be translated as the "call from above" or the "upward call" (ἄνω κλήσεως), but the point is made more explicitly a few verses on: "our citizenship is in heaven, and it is from there that we are expecting a Savior, the Lord Jesus Christ. He will transform the body of our humiliation that it may be conformed to the body of his glory" (vv. 20-21).

Such heavenly hopes constitute one of basic features of the doctrine of vocation in the New Testament, especially in the Epistles. We have just seen the theme of the heavenly "call" from Philippians 3:14, but the concept of calling is frequently used in the New Testament in the context of the Christian hope. Ephesians 1:18 speaks of the "hope to which he has called you, . . . the riches of his glorious inheritance among the saints"; 1 Thessalonians 2:12 speaks of the God "who calls you into his own kingdom and glory." The point of 2 Thessalonians 2:14 is similar: "he called you through our proclamation of the good news, so that you may obtain the glory of our Lord Jesus Christ." The expression "heavenly calling" itself appears in Hebrews 3:1, consistent with the enormous emphasis placed on the "heavenly sanctuary" later in the epistle as the location of true Christian worship. Finally, 1 Peter 5:10 speaks of "the God of all grace, who has called you to his eternal glory in Christ."

This list of citations, drawn from a wide variety of sources, though also far from complete — for there is more direct and especially indirect evidence to support our contention — illustrates how the idea of the call to heaven is a core concern of the theology of the New Testament. It is not merely a peripheral notion tacked on externally to a set of teachings that can easily survive without it; it is integral to the whole.

A variety of factors, however, have combined to make the hope of heaven, and the whole notion of the heavenly calling, a questionable ideal in modern times. The critique of transcendence associated with the this-worldliness of modern thought, its pragmatic and anti-speculative character, has already been mentioned. This is perhaps the most fundamental factor. It is also related to the whole character of Western thought since the mid-nineteenth century, which has sought truth and value in this world of life and nature rather than in the other world of transcendence, the realm of the spirit as traditionally conceived. Marx and Freud are two of the most important prophets of this tendency: for Marx, religion is an opiate precisely because of the heavenly dream that deflects attention away from the here-and-now; for Freud, religion is a murky reflection of bizarre, irrational events in the distant past of either the human species as a whole or the individual subject, which have first to be understood and then left behind. Allied with such development has been the general atmosphere of modern culture, to which the *relevance* of a heavenly order, should one exist, is questionable. If heaven represents anything, it is the sphere of the absolute source and goal of human existence, the absolute that ultimately renders the finitude of the world ultimately undesirable, or at best provisional. But modern thought sees itself as having no need of such an absolute. Its values are human constructs, and its truths are this-worldly: relative, contextual, and linguistic. This is not a soil in which to grow the hope of heaven.

In the light of all this, it is striking that the tendency to view the doctrine of vocation as if it were a question of secular occupation first arose at the turn of the twentieth century, being associated especially with the names of Weber and Troeltsch. Admittedly, as these men pointed out, there were precedents of a sort in English Calvinism, but the approach characteristic of Weber and Troeltsch is one that we have had reason to reject. Classical Protestantism never committed itself to the view that the Christian doctrine of vocation was fundamentally a question of secular work. If nothing else, its attachment to the Bible as the Word of God preserved it from such a reductionist approach; for, as we have seen, the Christian calling in the Bible is very much a religious rather than a secular concept, with a heavenly rather than a this-worldly frame of reference. This is certainly the case in Calvin's theology. For his part, Luther can be found, once one takes adequate account of the sources, to hold that earthly "standing" is more than simply a mode of life through which God's creative work continues. For one's standing in Luther's theology can also have a redemptive function. Through it, the "old man" of sin can be crucified: by serving the needs of one's fellow men and women, one is able to die to self and live to God. The latter theme is basic to Luther's well-known "theology of the cross." In fact, we must judge it never to be far from his central concern.

It would not be easy for contemporary Christianity to regain a vital sense of the significance of the heavenly calling. There are few theologians who would wish to see it, and the Christian church in the West as a whole is perhaps too wrapped up in the characteristic forms of contemporary culture to escape their present hold on the religious imagination. Nevertheless, there is a residual concern for life after death in our religious culture, and the case for a renewal of the doctrine of transcendence in some form is very strong from a theological point of view. We are, after all, concerned with *God* here, and not with the world — though to be concerned with God is also necessarily to be concerned with the world that God has created and redeemed. But there is little doubt that a return to what Karl Barth called the "Godness of God" is still very much needed in theology. With such a return will come a renewed concern for transcendence. Thus paradise may, after all, be regained.

Religious Vocation

Closely allied with the idea of the call to fellowship with God is the idea of religious vocation within the church. Traditional Catholic theology, for example, speaks both of the general vocation to supernatural life, which is God's call to accept the gift of himself, and of the specific "religious" and "clerical" vocations within the church. The religious vocation is to a life that pursues perfection as its special obligation, generally within an established religious order, while the clerical vocation is to ecclesiastical office and the hierarchy. With the notable exception of the recent *Catechism of the Catholic Church,* which focuses for the most part on the general vocation of Christians, the question of religious and clerical life has predominated in Catholic discussion of the doctrine of vocation. For my part, I am using the expression "religious vocation" in a looser, and perhaps more "Protestant" sense to refer to any ministry in the church, but I do not wish to exclude discussion of a vocation to life in religious community. This will be discussed later.

The theology of ministry is a vast and complex subject; quite apart from questions such as those of Episcopal versus Presbyterian order, the nature and limits of authority, and the sociological-anthropological parallels to Christian institutional ministry, there is the whole question of what has come to be known as the "ministry of the whole people of God." Not all of these matters can even be touched upon here. We begin our necessarily selective account, however, with Luther once more. As in other areas, Luther is very much a touchstone for the theology of ministry. Particularly in his early theology, he developed a revolutionary approach that went to the root of the whole conception of ecclesiastical office. In the end, even he abandoned it, but this does not mean that it has outlived its theological usefulness. Luther once again has much to say to us.

We have already encountered the idea of the priesthood of all believers in Luther's theology, in connection with his denial of the medieval distinction between the spiritual and temporal estate. In Luther's theology, therefore, the idea of the priesthood of all believers is not primarily about ministry as such. It is concerned instead with the relationship that all have with Christ by virtue of baptism. There are, Luther teaches, no separate levels of grace, one for the clergy and one for the laity. Luther's objective is to break down the "walls" of status and standing before God that were introduced into medieval theology and to replace the medieval conception with a more evangelical understanding. The priesthood of all believers is the primary conception Luther used to bring about this shift of perspective: we are *all* priests, he claims, because we all have the same relation to Christ. What constitutes the church is the gospel of forgiveness, in which all alike are sinners acceptable to God in Christ. The fact that all Christians may approach God on this basis means that there is no need for a select intermediary to do the work on our behalf: all are priests in this sense, for all have been forgiven and incorporated into Christ. The idea of the priesthood of all believers, then, is rooted in Luther's claim that all Christians are of the spiritual estate (*Stand*).

In Luther's early theology, however, such concepts come to have a bearing on the theology of ministry also. First of all, because of the common priesthood and the denial of the medieval view that some are priests and some are not, it is no longer possible to conceive of ministerial office as involving a different *status* from the rest of the church, but only a different *office* or *work* within the context of the priesthood of all. Luther's claim is that out of the common priesthood, leaders may be chosen by all and delegated to fulfill certain responsibilities on behalf of the rest: all have the right and the duty to preach the gospel, to celebrate the sacraments, and to pronounce absolution, but because we live in a world in which labor is divided, and because of the need for good order, it is best that some people be appointed to fulfill the priestly responsibilities of the whole people of God on a regular basis.

Luther's early theology of ministry has a number of interesting features. First of all, since an appointment to ministerial office involves no fundamental theological change in the minister's relationship to Christ or to the church, the ministerial office can be temporary. Second, the authority of the minister derives very clearly from the common priesthood of the church, for it is the church that delegates its authority to the minister chosen. Therefore, ministerial authority does not derive from God directly, but only from God *through the church,* conceived as the whole company of believers. Luther's conception at this point is basically "congregational" in character: the church he has in mind is the local church, and the situation in view, as often as not, relates to the early shortage of ministers in the nascent Lutheran movement. He writes, for example, with a view to the position of the Lutheran company of believers living under a Catholic bishop, who will obviously be unwilling to appoint a Lutheran to lead that particular flock in the diocese. In such a situation, the common priesthood legitimates the appointment *by the congregation* of one of its members to fulfill the sacramental and liturgical responsibilities entrusted to all. The minister, therefore, as conceived in Luther's early theology, does not rule with divine authority over the congregation. The role of the minister, rather, can only properly be conceived as that of the *servant* — which is, of course, the true meaning of the word "ministry" in any case.

The contrast between Luther and Calvin on this point could scarcely be clearer. For Luther, the will of God comes to the individual through the neighbor — in this case, through the neighbor in the form of the Christian community. One discerns one's calling because others tell of it. "You are needed here" — this statement from the neighbor, in effect, becomes the voice of God, though we must add that Luther sees this as taking place under the authority of the Word. No one is needed in ministry who does not believe the gospel or who is ill-informed, and Christian character must be taken into account as well. What is surprising in Luther's early theology, however, is the extent to which all of this is simply presupposed and subsumed under the ruling idea of the priesthood of all believers. Despite his tendency toward pessimism regarding human nature, the early Luther is supremely confident about the Christian standing of the common man and woman; guided by the Word of God, which is open to all, the ordinary Christian possesses, in principle, the authority to appoint or to depose a minister.

Calvin actually passes over "the secret calling" (*Institutes*, 4.3.11), which is in fact at the heart of all that he has to say about the Christian ministry, but the call as he understands it comes directly from God — though it is to be tested and ratified by the church before ordination. Calvin devotes most of his attention to the organizational features of ministry and to its dogmatic presuppositions in what is sometimes called the Reformed doctrine of "accommodation." Because we are physical, social creatures, we require physical, outward helps to achieve our intended goal in the service of God. Furthermore, because the world is God's creature, he deals with us even in the sphere of grace in terms that we can bear: he does not speak directly from heaven, but through his appointed channels. These are the ministers, who speak for him and even "represent his person" (*Institutes,* 4.3.1). This is no "low" theology of ministry; as John Milton once remarked dryly about the Calvinism of Commonwealth England, "New Presbyter is but old Priest writ large" (*On the New Forcers of Conscience under the Long Parliament).* The point was more than philological; the logic of Calvin's position is indeed very similar in a number of important respects to the logic of classical Catholic theologies of ministry. Ministers, for example, hold the church together, govern it, and have divine authority over it; they are appointed by God, as we have seen, as his representatives; they cannot be deposed by a congregation. In fact, no mention is made of the priesthood of all believers in the whole of Calvin's discussion of ministry. We may with some justice surmise that it is even deliberately excluded from consideration. There is no doubt that Calvin's theology of ministry led to a more stable ecclesiastical organization than was possible on the basis of early Lutheran theology. No doubt it is to this extent a stronger position theologically. But it is also less interesting, less dazzling, less capable of inspiring positive action and development. It is likely for this reason that much popular Calvinism has tended to adopt the Lutheran doctrine of the priesthood of all believers over the head, as it were, of Calvin himself, and to assimilate the Calvinist doctrine partially to the Lutheran.

The Call to Ministry

As to the question of discerning the call, there is again much help to be found in Luther's theology. A call to ministry is first and foremost, for example, a call to service rather than to lordship: the very word "ministry" (διακονία) denotes lowly service in the New Testament. There is much in Jesus' teaching to support such a view. "Whoever wants to be first must be last of all and servant of all" (Mark 9:35). What is most attractive about Luther's vision is that it is concern for the neighbor that leads to shouldering responsibility for his or her spiritual welfare. However, there is the possibility of the loss of a sense of direct calling by God in this more mediated doctrine of calling, and this has to be recognized. There are also attendant risks; the early Lutheran doctrine looks very like the procedures of Western democracies: Would there be ecclesiastical parties vying for popular support were Luther's early theology really to be put into practice? I shall suggest below that there are situations in which Luther's suggestions might be put to good use today; but on the grand scale, I would be inclined to say that we know too much about the failures of our democratic system to want it to be widely mirrored in our churches. The craving for power and the Christian doctrine of ministry do not mix well. Anyone, then, who contemplates a call to the Christian ministry would do well to consider the more fundamental issue at stake in the Lutheran conception: Is it the need of the neighbor that compels one to take this course in life? Or would it be better to serve the neighbor in some other capacity? This, combined with prayerful consideration of the divine calling and a measured response by the church itself in selecting its candidates for ministry, would go far toward achieving balance in these matters. And a balanced approach is perhaps the best that we can hope for: practical wisdom will always be content with a certain amount of ambiguity.

God does, however, call some to service in special ways in the Bible, and while the contemporary preference for a greater measure of mutuality and co-operation in matters pertaining to the work of the church is in itself a laudable thing, it is perhaps more humanly and theologically responsible to expect God to continue to call some to serve in this way in the present as well. Social organizations require clear leadership, and the church is no exception. Furthermore, throughout the

Bible, God seems to do his work through selected agents much more than through collective groups. It is really implausible to think that were all to be equally accepted and affirmed within the church, and all given their say, the whole would spontaneously move forward in a seamless web of unity and peace. The contemporary ethic of accepting others and of attempting to make room for their views has its limits, both for the confessional position of the Christian church and for its polity. The call must therefore continue to be a living concern within the church, which requires ministry in order to function properly.

Ministry, however, is always contextual, and the sense of the call will almost certainly always be geared to some special context, to some situation or group of people, or even to some place. "Now there are varieties of gifts, but the same Spirit; and there are varieties of services (διακονιῶν), but the same Lord; and there are varieties of activities, but it is the same God who activates all of them in everyone. To each is given the manifestation of the Spirit for the common good" (1 Cor. 12:4-7). The text in its original setting refers to the well-known *charismata* in evidence in the Corinthian church, but it applies by extension to the work of ministry generally. What distinguishes one ministry from another, what individuates at this point, are the unique gifts and sense of calling of the minister and the specific situation in which he or she works. Thus the specific needs of people in some situation or location can be an important factor in a sense of vocation: they can, in short, help to define who the neighbor is for whom love is to be shown and to whom service in the name of Christ will be offered.

Ministry as Service

The emphasis on service is extremely important, for the ultimate theological basis of ministry lies in the ministry of Christ, who came "not to be served but to serve, and to give his life a ransom for many" (Mark 10:45). This fact alone ought to be enough to condemn the widespread tendency within the Christian church to see ministry in terms of authority rather than service. The temptation is understandable; if God is the sovereign Lord of creation and redemption, if the church is his chosen instrument for fulfilling his will on earth, and if the minister is called to represent his authority in the world and in the church, then the language of power becomes something obvious and even necessary. Someone who is powerless cannot truly represent an authoritative Lord. We need to ask, however, whether the view of God as the alternatively fascinating or terrible plenitude of absolute power bears any relation to the God revealed in the gospel, the God who is love, who is revealed by the crucified one, and whose authority waits upon the faith and obedience of his people.

In fact, the church has no ministry of its own; its ministry is Christ's. His command to go out into the world with the gospel is the origin of ministry in the church; he gives his gift of the Holy Spirit so that the church will have the resources to fulfill its charge. Ministry is thus given to the church; it comes from outside, namely, from the risen Lord as the continuation of his ministry. It is not something self-generated. Grounding ministry in this way in the ministry of Christ, however, has important implications. Jesus' ministry, for example, is a trinitarian event. He is the one sent by the Father into the world and anointed by the Spirit to fulfill his work. As one sent, he exercises his ministry in obedience. He comes as the Lord over sin and death, but he exercises his lordship as the obedient Son who seeks not his own glory but the glory of the Father who sent him. What is astonishing about this is that the glory of the Father is realized in Jesus' fellowship with the sinner and the outcast, with the marginalized and the Godless. Christian ministry, if it is to be Christlike, must reflect these same structures. Above all, it will reflect Christ's servanthood. His is a lordship that is found not in the wielding of worldly power but in self-emptying love.

It is true that the church also needs to be seen as a messianic community in which we have a share in Christ's lordship, and even a share in his authority over sin and death. In ministry, we proclaim the word of forgiveness and reconciliation, bearing witness to the salvation that has been brought to pass through Christ. But the idea of sharing in Christ's lordship is also a dangerous thing, for it carries with it the temptation to conform to earthly models of authority. It is in this way that worldly power has so often come to be seen as an appropriate expression of Christ's power, whether by the medieval popes who behaved as political despots, or by the local parson whose chief ambition was to please the parish aristocrats. Over against this, it is a healthy corrective to remember that the New Testament uses no authority words to describe or to denote the role of office-bearers in the church. Authority words would be such terms as "rule" (ἀρχή), but such terms are used almost always in the New Testament to refer to the powers *opposed* to Christ's own authority. The authority of Christ and the thought of the New Testament stand over against these: although Christ has rule ascribed to him, there is never any suggestion that he has assumed earthly forms of authority over the political and social order, but rather that he has *overcome* them. In the New Testament, neither are Christian leaders spoken of in this way.

In total contrast to models of earthly power, the only New Testament word used generically of church leaders denotes not what authoritarian figures do in political or social life, but what servants do. The New Testament word that we have already encountered is *diakonia,* the generic term in the New Testament for ministry, which denotes the humble service of a slave. To conceive of leadership in this way was a total innovation in the primitive Christian church; nothing like it had ever been seen before in previous models of leadership. It had its origins, of course, in the radical overthrow of preconceived religious ideas that was heralded by the coming of Christ himself and by his life and teaching. The Lord who washed the disciples' feet is the same one who commanded that we are also to wash one another's feet (John 13:13-14). Above all, the Lord who submitted to crucifixion for the sake of the church demands an analogous response on the part of those who claim to follow him.

It goes almost without saying, of course, that this vision of leadership, pioneered by Christ himself, proved too much for the church to live with. Increasingly, models of ministry were developed in abstraction from the servanthood of Christ, attempting instead to ground the church's ministry in Christ's heavenly status as the eternal Word and Wisdom of the Father, the bearer of his authority and of his glory. This is reflected in what is arguably one of the great tragedies of Christian history: the separation that has been introduced between *diakonia* and other forms of ministry. The threefold distinction between bishops, priests, and deacons is one clear example of this, but one of the worst appears in a variety of Protestant traditions that define deacons as those ministers who are given responsibility over temporal matters. The basis for this is the passage in Acts 6 in which seven "deacons" are appointed to fulfill such tasks, in clear distinction from what the preachers and the evangelists, the apostles, were doing. In fact, Acts 6 does not use the word *diakonia* of the so-called "deacons" at all; rather, the word is used as a description of what the apostles and those entrusted with temporal responsibilities were all alike doing. Their work is just one *more* form of *diakonia*. Paul, similarly, regularly describes his apostolic office as *diakonia* (Rom. 11:13), and he seems to say that the function of the whole church is the *diakonia* of reconciliation. But this is a costly business; it requires a constant sacrifice of love and can never be fulfilled at a lordly distance from the sin and pain of the world. Above all, what must never be forgotten is the fact that Christ's actual lordship was expressed in lowly service. For our part, we need to be on our guard against becoming venerable, reverend lords, and we must retain the attitude, the appearance, and the reality of servanthood.

Lay Ministry

The great sponsoring text in the New Testament for the "ministry of the whole people of God" must be Ephesians 4:12, which speaks of how the risen Christ gave gifts to the church — apostles, prophets, evangelists, pastors, and teachers — "to equip the saints for the work of ministry." This translation from the New Revised Standard Version is paralleled widely in contemporary translations of the Bible (witness, for example, the New International Version's "to prepare God's people for works of service," and even the Catholic Jerusalem Bible's almost inexplicable "so that the saints together make a unity in the work of service"), but it differs in one significant respect from the King James Version's "For the perfecting of the saints, for the work of the ministry, for the edifying of the body of Christ." Apart from the obvious matter of vocabulary, the key difference lies in the comma separating the first two clauses in the older translation. One of my teachers, Professor John C. O'Neill, taught me the significance of this. There is a great deal of difference between saying that apostles, prophets, pastors, and teachers were given to equip the saints as a whole for *their* work of ministry, and saying that they were given to perfect the saints — that is to say, that these leaders were themselves given to do the work of ministry within the church. The Greek text supports either reading, but there is no doubt that it is contemporary sensibility as much as the text itself that dictates how the translators tend to construe it today.

Ephesians 4:12, therefore, may well be a questionable proof-text. Nevertheless, I am not inclined to attempt to undermine the case for lay ministry; I am myself a lay minister within my Church of Scotland parish, sharing leadership in a new church initiative with a number of other lay and ordained people. I have also worked on various occasions in pastoral charges of the United Church of Canada as a lay minister involved in worship, preaching, administration, and pastoral care. My own most positive experiences of Christian worship and witness have come in contexts in which the ministry of all is taken most seriously. But a coherent theological case for lay ministry remains to be adequately formulated.

There is no scope to provide a full treatment here, but a basic case for lay ministry can be outlined. Let me begin with a plea for theological reflection. Let us imagine a church in numerical decline, under financial pressure, and hidebound in a rather hierarchical theology of ministry. In sparsely populated rural areas especially, where historically there have been local churches in virtually every hamlet, but where in our hypothetical situation numbers and givings have fallen off for some years, ecclesiastical practice will frequently be to close and amalgamate local churches wherever possible. The manner in which this would be likely to occur is significant. Upon the retirement or transfer of a *minister* from a parish, an ecclesiastical court will deem it necessary that for financial reasons, a church must close. The idea that a church might function without an ordained minister on hand week by week will be rejected as unworkable. Little progress will accordingly have been made on the introduction of a "bi-vocational" model of ministry (the precedent being the apostle Paul, who earned his own living by manual labor while preaching the gospel in Corinth). Nor, correspondingly, will significant moves have been made toward providing adequate resources of literature on ideas for worship, selections from commentaries on the set readings for the church year, and the like, so that capable local people might use them in lay ministry to keep their beloved churches open.

This is, of course, more than merely a hypothetical situation; it actually reflects widespread practice within the Presbyterian tradition in Scotland at least, as well as in a variety of other ecclesiastical traditions on the international scene. But now let us ask a question: Might not an impartial observer, seeing such developments, validly be led to conclude not merely that on such a view the church cannot exist without a professional minister, but that the church exists as much for the sake of the maintenance of the ordained ministry as vice versa? We are, at this point, it needs to be said, a long way from the New Testament understanding of the minister as servant. A new vision of the possibilities for lay ministry, however, would go a great way toward solving such problems, toward healing some of the alienation of people from religion (for many are alienated because of such practices), and toward helping to keep the life of many local Christian communities viable. There is also obvious scope here for the development of insights from congregationalist traditions within Protestantism. It is interesting to note that, within the Presbyterian tradition, such a doctrine of ministry is probably best seen in practice, not in Europe or in North America, but among Presbyterians in rural Africa, where the religious and social role of the "elder" is generally taken very seriously indeed!

Part of the problem that needs to be overcome if a theology of lay ministry is to take hold is the language and conceptuality that prevails in so much discussion of ministry. It is fundamental to a number of Christian traditions that some are said to share in Christ's ministry in a way that others do not. On such a view, the church is not a society of equals in which all have the same rights. It is a society of unequals, not merely because of the distinction between the clergy and the laity, but more specifically because power from God is given to some to sanctify, teach, and govern, while to others it is not. Such a view is sometimes associated with the rather disturbing and reactionary *fin-de-siècle* Catholicism of Vatican I, but in fact, with due allowances for the planing off of a hairsbreadth here or there, it fairly represents the standard furnishings of the theology of ministry in most of the Christian traditions.

The language of layperson and cleric itself can be characterized as a language of "apartheid," and as such it is very revealing. Sadly, it has a long history. As early as the second century, there is evidence that the church began to call one of its members, the leader in worship and especially the bishop, a priest (ἱερεύς or *sacerdos*). The New Testament, by contrast, never uses this word to designate Christian leaders, but solely to speak of Christ. Along with such usage, furthermore, came the distinction between the priestly clergy and the people. The word for the people was λαός, from which our word "laity" derives, whereas the corresponding word for the priest was κλῆρος, from which we derive our word "clergy." The word κλῆρος means "chosen one," and underlying it is the idea of some being chosen by God, in distinction from "the people." Certainly as early as Cyprian (ca. 200-258) in the West, the idea had developed that the clergy have a relationship with Christ that differs from that of other people: the clergy have become a separate class of human mediators, in the sense that without them there is no sacramental access to God. Over against such long-standing usage, however, we need to set the clear teaching of the New Testament: "you are a chosen race, a royal priesthood, a holy nation, God's own people, in order that you may proclaim the mighty acts of him who called you out of darkness into his marvelous light" (1 Pet. 2:9). The "you" refers to the whole people of God and allows no distinction of class or of being.

In the light of such biblical teaching, an alternative ecclesiological position is required in order to redress the long-standing imbalance in the Christian doctrine of ministry. The context is important, for our theology of ministry will reflect our general ecclesiology. I wish to suggest that one way in which to develop a framework for a theology of lay ministry is to distinguish between ecclesiology as seen "from above" and as seen "from below." This corresponds to the christological distinction that has passed into the common currency of twentieth-century Christian thought: "Christology from above" represents the divine movement into the world in Jesus; "Christology from below" represents the movement of the human Jesus toward the Father in faith and obedience, together with the standard set of questions surrounding the status of the "Jesus of history" that can be raised in our theology. In the same way, and even by way of strict theological method, one can say the same of the doctrine of the church. On the one hand, the church is the Spirit's creation in the world, a divine institution brought into being by the whole trinitarian outreach in grace, which culminates in the church as the ark of salvation. This is the church seen "from above." Ecclesiology "from below," however, is no less theological. Here we are concerned with the church, not as institution, but as event, and specifically with the church as the event that happens when and where the Holy Spirit is at work among the people of God. The church is thus conceivable as a community of saints, in which people love God and serve humanity, and in which people have a variety of gifts that can work together for the common good. This view allows for a *charismatic* doctrine of ministry as opposed to an *institutional* doctrine of ministry. On such a view, ministry is located where the charisms are, among the whole people of God, the "chosen race" and "royal priesthood" of 1 Peter.

This kind of vision of the church and of its ministry is

pregnant with possibilities. Both aspects, however, are required for a full understanding. Just as in Christology a complete understanding of Jesus requires some attempt to grasp both his divinity and his humanity, so our doctrine of the church requires both an institutional and a charismatic line of approach. In fact, we need to draw together both aspects. Even if we affirm the institutional character of the church as the "mother of believers," for example, or as the creation of the Holy Spirit, the terminus of the great descending movement "from the Father, through the Son, in the Holy Spirit" that structures the divine economy of salvation, we are nevertheless left to ask why the church exists as such. For it is not an end in itself. The church as institution, or as the creation of the Spirit endowed with divine authority, really exists for the sake of something else: so that there can be a community of saints who love and serve God, and so continue the mission of Christ in the world. This latter approach to ecclesiology requires a charismatic theology: in it is found a movement of love and faith from below that reaches simultaneously toward God and toward the world that God loves. If it is true that without the institution the charismatic model of the church begins to look anarchic, disorganized, and ultimately sectarian, it is also true that without the charismatic reality of the church the institution becomes decadent, self-satisfied, and lifeless. In fact, we may say that while the charismatic model needs the institutional for balance and maturity, the institutional exists only for the sake of the charismatic — that is, only so that a genuine community of love and faith can exist, a true "people of God."

We may apply the same line of reasoning, I wish to suggest, to our understanding of Christian ministry. As an institutional reality, the church requires stable and perhaps permanent leadership. But the idea that this constitutes the whole of the Christian ministry is obviously mistaken. In fact, we may say that the institutional ministry exists so that there can be the charismatic ministry of the whole people of God, a community in which love, for example, is a common concern, and in which to be a "servant" is seen as the common task and goal. Charismatic ministry, seen from this perspective, is not a matter of a pietistic and subjective quest for supernatural experience. Fundamentally, it is concerned with continuing the mission of Christ, with finding identity in the calling with which we are called: to love God and to serve the neighbor. To be God's servants, then, means to feed the hungry and to clothe the naked, to heal the sick and to visit the imprisoned — in fact, it must mean this before it means anything else. As such, it is a concept closely related to our own treatment of the doctrine of vocation.

The Secular "Calling"

One of my friends insists that God called him to be a fireman. His case is interesting, for it illustrates a number of the central themes of this book. In the first place, there is the fact that in his work he is able to do good. The destruction of life and property brought on by fire is clearly something that needs to be fought, so much so that there is frequently good moral reason for acts of heroism in the fire service. Society rightly looks up to those who carry out this work. But my friend's sense of calling to the fire service involves more than this. Because of shift work and the sometimes long periods spent in his fire station, he was able to undertake part-time study for the "auxiliary ministry" of the Church of Scotland. This is a recent and welcome initiative under which someone in secular employment can work in conjunction with a minister in a local parish on a part-time basis, without payment beyond expenses. There is a greatly reduced period of academic training before ordination, but following ordination the auxiliary minister is able to carry out a full range of ministerial duties, short of taking on a parish of his or her own. My friend's work in the fire service not only enabled him to undertake these studies but also provided the context for a unique ministry to the firemen of the Lothian and Borders Fire Brigade in Scotland. He visits the injured and provides pastoral care in difficult situations: dealing with tragedy is often extremely difficult for members of the fire service. In addition to this, he works a set number of hours each week in the parish.

I have suggested in this book that the Christian calling is fundamentally to be understood in terms of the two great commandments, which are to love the Lord God with the whole self and to love the neighbor as oneself. My friend's work as a fireman has allowed him to fulfill both: his love for God has found expression in his work in ministry, while the love of neighbor is fulfilled both in his work as a fireman and in his ministerial role in a variety of contexts. I am, however, unable to agree with his claim that God called him to be a *fireman*. The call of God in the Bible is the call to do something that can be directly characterized as religious in quality — for example, some action to which the Word of God directs us. It would be more accurate, therefore, to speak of the calling that his work as a fireman allowed him to fulfill: to show love, to do good, to train for ministry, and to work in Christian service in the church and in the workplace.

At the beginning of this book, I made mention of the piety in which I was myself reared, according to which God's plan for each life extends to such details of life as career choices. I have sought to develop an alternative vision, one that allows a certain freedom to the creature before God to make its own choices and way, but one within which the general contours of living uprightly and seeking the good of the neighbor are given by God. From this standpoint, the secular world provides opportunities for a Christian vocation that are very real. The ordinary responsibilities a man or a woman bears in the world are, one might say, the "location" in which the Christian calling is lived. To this extent, then, our old friend Luther was right: the mother fulfills her calling in showing love for her children; the milkmaid in doing her job well; the woodworker in finishing a house or a chair in such a way as to be useful to others. One can fulfill the Christian calling by showing charity to colleagues at work, by "loving justice and showing kindness" as best one can on the shop floor or in the boardroom. And in situations of "hard labor," where each minute is spent doing something personally disagreeable, something for which one is unsuited, a person can nevertheless earn bread for others for whom he or she cares: this, too, can be a calling, for there is a moral, and even a sacred meaning, in that as well.

CHAPTER 7

Love

"The Greatest of These"

If I had to distill the whole of this little book into a single brief sentence, it would be this: "The Christian calling is to love." The ideal of love alone can adequately reflect the whole of the teaching of Jesus and the ethic of the kingdom of God; it is also love alone that can provide an adequate answer to the question, "What will I do with my life?" Love, of course, can be expressed in many ways, from the intimate love of a parent, to the responsible and at times exasperated dedication of the schoolteacher, or in a healthy patriotism, expressed in the kind of love of neighbor that leads to service within the local, regional, or national community. Love is manifested in moneys given for disaster relief, in work in the voluntary sector, and in cutting a neighbor's lawn while he is away. It is the most ordinary of virtues, but it is also the one thing most worth living for.

Religious faith, of course, involves many things. There is the daily and weekly devotional practice, the informal or formal worship that is its most obvious sign and seal on human life.

It involves a set of beliefs, a worldview which serves to order human life, and from which liturgical practice is drawn. Religion involves both an outward embodiment and an inward disposition, a spirituality hidden from view and often difficult to express in words. But the Christian religion is most fully and most concretely expressed in love.

One of the most extraordinary passages in the New Testament is the so-called "hymn to love" of 1 Corinthians 13. It is extraordinary for its beauty and simplicity, but most of all for the fact that it was written by the apostle Paul. For here it is none other than Paul, the apostle of justification by faith, or even of justification by faith *alone* if Luther is to be believed, who tells us that greater than all else — greater even than faith — is love. "And now, faith, hope, and love abide, these three; and the greatest of these is love" (1 Cor. 13:13). Nor is this a momentary lapse, a slip of the tongue or of the pen on Paul's part, for the passage as a whole begins with the claim that having "all faith," even a faith that can remove mountains, is nothing without love. Admittedly, the whole passage is highly rhetorical, sandwiched as it is between two highly emotive discussions of the spiritual gifts of the Corinthian church. But that it is to be found in the Pauline corpus of the New Testament at all is itself highly remarkable.

Although Paul uses the ideal of love as the key to ethics, the Pauline view of love is ultimately rooted in nothing less than the love of God that came into the world in Jesus Christ. The typical Pauline word for it is "grace" (χάρις): "For you know the grace of our Lord Jesus Christ, that though he was rich, yet for your sakes he became poor, so that you through his poverty might become rich" (2 Cor. 8:9, NIV). But Paul also frequently speaks more plainly of the love of God: "God proves his love for us in that while we still were sinners Christ died for us" (Rom. 5:8). In this, as in other areas, the Pauline view is virtually identical to the Johannine: "Beloved, since God loved us so much, we also ought to love one another" (1 John 4:11). This same teaching is found on the lips of Jesus himself in the Gospel of John: "This is my commandment, that you love one another as I have loved you. No one has greater love than this, to lay down one's life for one's friends" (John 15:12-13). And this Pauline-Johannine perspective is also, of course, complemented by Jesus' own summary of the law in the synoptic Gospels, enjoining the love of God and the love of neighbor.

Love in Theology

Despite all of this, love is curiously absent from much theology. In Protestantism, for example, hostility to the Catholic tendency toward a doctrine of "justification by love" has typically led to resistance to the centrality of love in theology. Faith, accordingly, is the central theme of the Protestant tradition. In contemporary theology, by contrast, the wherewithal for a theology of love is provided by certain aspects of the theology of liberation, although the possibilities here are sometimes obscured by talk of praxis, which has very definite philosophical associations. Most of all, however, the idea of Christian love has been widely misrepresented and misunderstood in this century, not so much because of the debasing of love in popular culture through its association with ecstasy and its dissociation from morality, as because of the baleful influence on much popular Christianity of the Swedish Lutheran Anders Nygren. His influential book *Agape and Eros*[1] may not have been widely read by the people in the pews, but his views have been disseminated far and wide through the work of preachers and more popular Christian writers.

The extent to which Nygren's views have been popularized

1. Anders Nygren, *Agape and Eros,* trans. A. G. Hebert et al., 2 vols. (London: SPCK, 1932, 1938).

in the twentieth century is remarkable, especially given the nature of his position. At one point, for example, he claims as one of his fundamental theses that "The man whom God loves has not any value in himself. His value consists simply in the fact that God loves him" (I, p. 54). Otherwise, we would find ourselves in the curious position of saying either that human sin did not matter to God, or that human righteousness can earn favor with God, or that God can be affected by the activity of his creatures — in which case he is no longer impassible. All of these factors militate in one form or another in Nygren's theology against the notion that God's love should be a love of something good in his creatures. And yet, this is precisely the problem, for human beings as the objects of divine love are God's creation, part of that of which it is said, "God saw everything that he had made, and indeed, it was very good" (Gen. 1:31). Not even sin can wipe out the fundamental goodness of the person *as God's creature;* God's love for us, like human love, must be intrinsically related to the dignity of the human person.

Unfortunately, large numbers of Christians have been told in recent times that Christian love, *agape,* is only shown where love mirrors a divine *agape* that is totally unrelated to any value in its object. The fact is, however, that such a claim is both inconsistent with New Testament usage and theologically incoherent. In the New Testament, God "is" indeed *agape* (1 John 4:8), while at the same time God's love is indeed shown to the sinful and the faithless. This does not mean, however, that the word *agape* regularly refers to such selfless love in the New Testament. In fact, the situation is quite the reverse: "Do not love the world or the things in the world. The love of the Father is not in those who love the world" (1 John 2:15). According to this text, a person can love the world with *agape* and still be proud and lustful, knowing nothing of the quality of *God's* love. The case for a unique concept of *agape* as self-giving is, then, far from proven in the New Testament. Theologically, furthermore, although there is no doubt that Christian love is self-giving, it is not self-giving for no end. The whole point is that it recognizes the worth of what is loved: the neighbor is a creature of moral worth, one "for whom Christ died," who is, as such, the object of God's concern.

Nygren's position also had another unfortunate effect on the Christian conscience. According to Nygren, the fundamental characteristics of *agape* are opposed to all the fundamental characteristics of *eros;* the latter seeks the fulfillment of the self, whereas the former seeks simply to do good, without any reference to the worth of its object or to the fulfillment of the self. Now once again, there is no doubt that *self*-fulfillment is not the goal of Christian love, for it is genuinely centered on the other and on his or her fulfillment. On the other hand, there is absolutely nothing unchristian about seeking true fulfillment in the service of God: to quote Jesus, "those who lose their life for my sake will find it" (Matt. 16:25). The same point can be put another way, in keeping with another point of popular devotional wisdom: "You shall love your neighbor as yourself," says Jesus (Matt. 22:39), or again, in the Sermon on the Mount, "In everything do to others as you would have them do to you" (Matt. 7:12). But a sense of the worth of the self is the only thing that can make such commandments even intelligible. In order to love another, one must be able also to love oneself, but this will always be a hard thing to do in Nygren's theological world. It is, in the end, an intellectual system like many others, internally consistent and externally open to certain, at least, of the relevant facts, but nevertheless impossible to live in.

The question of vocation, "What will I do with my life?" is one that can be answered for the Christian only in terms of love, for love is the way of Christ himself, and the way of the God who sent him into the world. Ultimately, there is nothing else in theology worth knowing or clinging to; "God is love," proclaims 1 John 4:8, summing up in three little words what the entire vast corpus of Christian theology is really about. And yet, the point is often missed. Theology itself, we have heard again and again, is the *logos* of *theos,* the "knowledge of God." But what if its real content were not primarily intellectual but moral? What if its fundamental reference were not truth but relationship? What if theology, rightly conceived, were not knowledge in the first instance at all? At this point, the Christian theological tradition can easily fail us, and we are thrown back upon a more original, one might say also more authentic, experience of the God of Jesus Christ. Only the encounter with God, who is love, can mediate the sense of vocation as love in the world — love alone, whatever the cost. What will I do with my life? I will, above all else, follow the way of Christ.

Carrying the Cross

"If any want to become my followers, let them deny themselves and take up their cross and follow me" (Mark 8:34). People have no need to look far to find their cross, for on Jesus' lips such words mean one thing: giving up one's self for others. In its original context, Jesus' saying was a call to martyrdom for the sake of the gospel of the kingdom of God, or at the very least a call to be prepared for it. Such witness is rare nowadays, though it does take place and has often been embraced in Christian history. Nowadays, the call is generally to be understood as beckoning to something that seems more modest, to concrete service of some sort, on behalf of the neighbor or within the church. But such service as Christ commands never makes entirely modest demands: it is to love the enemy, to pray for the persecutor, to be the salt of the earth and the light of the world. Jesus himself is the "light of the world" according to the Johannine witness (John 8:12); but in this way, by continuing his work and mission, his followers, too, become the light of the world and are built into a city that cannot be hid (Matt. 5:14).

The carrying of the cross is often construed differently, of course. On the pastoral round, for example, a sentiment frequently encountered is that "we all have a cross to bear." The cross is here equated with suffering, and often with physical suffering or the infirmities of the aged. Now none of us would be so morally crass or theologically inept as to suggest to the arthritic or to the blind or to the depressed in such a situation that there is no fellowship in Christ's sufferings (Phil. 3:10), but it is true nevertheless that Christ's call is not to become arthritic or blind or depressed or marked in some other way by infirmity. This popular misunderstanding is also mirrored widely at present at the highest theological levels in the so-called "theology of the cross," according to which the core concern of Christian theology is suffering — both human and divine. In fact, when all is said and done — when fragments of the philosopher Hegel have been misconstrued, the problem of theodicy after Auschwitz cited, and the key question of the death of the Son of God probed — this view comes very close indeed to the conviction that "we all have a cross to bear" encountered at the pastoral level: participation in suffering is the human lot, but the human lot has been embraced by God. Yet the significance of the cross in Christian theology is something fundamentally positive: something aimed at redemption, at reconciliation, at justification, at salvation and restoration. Its meaning cannot legitimately be construed as consisting, without remainder, simply in the entanglement of God, too, in the human predicament.

Both Luther and Balthasar bring valuable perspectives to this theme of cross-bearing as basic to the Christian life. Luther sees the cross of Christian vocation in the fact that God calls us to serve our neighbor. In this way, the root of sin is addressed, for sinfulness is basically a form of selfishness in Luther's theology. In order to turn to the other in love, one has to die to self, and therefore to sin. Thus in the particular vocations, or "standings," by which God in his providence continues his creative activity, the purposes of redemption are also served. Luther's exploration of the doctrine of vocation leans heavily on Pauline ideas at this point. We are "crucified with Christ" (Gal. 2:19); just as Christ "died to sin, once for all" (Rom. 6:10), so we, too, must die to sin and live to serve God. What is most interesting about Lutheran theology at this point is the way in which all of this takes place in the ordinary sphere of life, amid the everyday responsibilities of the milkmaid. In fact, it is only the monk who has difficulty in fulfilling a vocation — precisely because, by withdrawing from the world in which people live, the monk shirks the commandment of Christ to show love to his neighbor.

The great weakness of Luther's doctrine of vocation, of course, is also the great weakness of Lutheran theology generally: for Luther, vocation belongs to the kingdom of law, but not to the kingdom of heaven. One's vocation on earth is therefore of no use in heaven; there, everything earthly is left behind, as good works especially are of no avail before God. The problem with this Lutheran doctrine of the "two kingdoms," however, is how the two can be related. If, in short, good works profit nothing as far as the kingdom of heaven is concerned, then why does God command them?

Balthasar's doctrine of vocation has the merit of overcoming this weakness; for on his account, the whole thrust of the saving act of God in the incarnation, life, death, and resurrection of Christ is toward the humanizing and personalizing of human beings "in Christ." They come to have a share in the mission of Christ *itself*, rather than in something secondary to it, or even something apparently "alien" to it (as would be true for the Lutheran conception). Thus the sharing of the mission of Christ, which was centered on the cross, involves the bearing of his cross. According to Balthasar, this is not something imposed by an angry God as the penalty for sin, either upon

Christ or upon his disciples, but the expression of a divine love, which must "annihilate, cauterize and excise (Heb. 4:12) all that is not love."[2] In the cross, we see "God himself being seared, even out of the very hellfire of sinful non-love itself, by the fire of divine love." The incorporation into Christ that lies at the heart of the Christian's mission, which involves spreading the reconciliation brought about by Christ, implies an entering into the mind of Christ by each believer, "that is, into his selflessness and his readiness to affirm others and forgive them — which can only come through self-sacrifice and a plunging into the breach on their behalf" (III, p. 121).

In the matter of vocation it is far less important for the Christian to find the particular mode of life by which he or she will "plunge into the breach" in and with Christ on behalf of others than that he or she does it *in some way*. It is not so much the particular "way" that matters, but the universal principle of love at stake in it all, the principle that is also revealed in Christ as the "way" of God. One does not, I have said, have to look far to find a cross to bear. But this cross, by which one is "crucified with Christ," is not a cross of physical suffering. It is, rather, the cross of self-giving, of bearing the sins of others for the sake of reconciliation, and thus the cross of love that must often entail suffering.

Community

When Luther argued that monastic life amounts to an abdication of one's responsibility to care for the neighbor, he effectively set a seal upon the ordinary world of human affairs as the one legitimate sphere of human community. No room was

2. Hans Urs von Balthasar, *Theo-Drama,* vol. III, trans. Graham Harrison (San Francisco: Ignatius Press, 1992), p. 119.

left in Luther's theology for the notion of ideal communities that might serve as models of Christian life. It was, perhaps, as much Luther's rather romantic early attachment to the Christian virtues of the ordinary man and woman as his lasting antipathy to monasticism and its perceived dangers that led to this conclusion. But the latter was the reason most frequently given: monasticism, he repeated over and over again, leads to an exaltation of works over faith — for why else would one flee from the world other than to earn favor with God, when all that is truly required is to hear the Word of the gospel with faith?

The abuses common within the religious orders of the late medieval era are well known and even notorious, and Luther was able to use public perception of the monasteries to good effect in his own popular writings. Unfortunately, however, Luther was deeply unfair to the ideal of religious community. It was, after all, the Augustinian order that largely educated him and gave him the opportunity to teach; it was precisely in this context that he was able to develop his own theology of justification by faith. Moreover, Luther himself was greatly indebted to certain of his religious superiors for his own spiritual development, and in particular to John Staupitz, the Vicar-General of his order, the man who first induced Luther to pursue his studies and to lecture on the Bible. Staupitz, who rejected the nominalist philosophy that lay at the heart of late medieval religion, also introduced Luther to a more satisfactory way of understanding the grace of God. "If Dr. Staupitz had not helped me out . . . I should have been swallowed up and left in hell," Luther once remarked.[3] Such tribute perhaps signals an unconscious sense of debt to the monastic tradition on Luther's part; but if so, it is a sense that

3. Quoted in Gordon Rupp, *The Righteousness of God* (London: Hodder and Stoughton, 1953), p. 118.

otherwise went unacknowledged at the public level in Luther's theology.

One of the obvious reasons for this was that monastic life in Luther's time had largely ceased to serve its intended function as a model of the Christian life. Apart from the sheer corruption of the religious ideal in some monasteries, Luther came to see the whole phenomenon of monastic life as a model of what the Christian life, understood in the Bible, is *not* about. The monasteries had become signs of justification by works, in short, whereas the gospel proclaims justification by faith. Rather than standing over against the world as a sign of the kingdom of God, therefore, the monasteries had become instruments of the devil, by which the consciences of the simple were entrapped and by which those who sought salvation were led astray. This is really what lies at the heart of Luther's rejection and denunciation of monasticism.

This does not, however, mean that Luther himself, and the Protestant Reformation that succeeded him, are necessarily committed to individualism, as if by default. The accusation of individualism is frequently made but cannot really be sustained. First of all, Luther insists that the responsibilities that one bears in the ordinary human community are a religious vocation, and nothing less than that. No suggestion is ever made that one can serve God by self-absorption. The Reformation scholar Gordon Rupp once went so far as to claim that some presentations of the "Lutheran" principle of private judgment really amount to what Martin Luther understood by "original sin" (*Righteousness of God,* p. 312). Second, Luther and the whole of the classical Reformation movement are totally committed to the church as the communion of saints: it is only within the church that sins are remitted, for it is among God's people, where the gifts of God are shared and where the Word of God and the sacraments are found, that God himself is at work.

Thus it is in the context of community that the Christian vocation is found and fulfilled, even in classical Protestantism. Today, however, it is more difficult to sympathize with the Reformation critique of the ideal of a religious community apart from the world. If one of the chief functions of the monastery in its original setting was to be a sign to the world that it is possible to live for something higher than wealth or power or sex, or even than one's daily bread, then might it not be possible to argue again that in a post-Christian world, the religious community once again has a role to play? This is a question that most of Protestant theology has never really addressed, but we need to recognize that whereas the Reformers themselves tended simply to assume that the visible church and society are coterminous, we are certainly no longer in such a position. In this context, might it not be appropriate to see religious community as a sign to the world of what the human vocation really is?

The nature of this community, of course, will be open to discussion, and to new possibilities. The church, for example, is already in principle a religious community, though its real character is seldom fully realized. One hour spent in the fellowship of other Christians on a Sunday morning, plus an evening a month in committee, does not yet constitute a true common life with other believers. But it is a start, and it is undoubtedly the most basic of all Christian community. There will, however, be some people who sense a beckoning to something more than this, or who need it for a time in their lives, or who wish to spend the rest of their lives in a closer religious fellowship. For these, there is no substitute for some version of the classical ideal of Christian religious community. Nowadays, we might envision communities of men and women, such as we see in the Iona Community in Scotland, which has drawn young and old, Catholic and Protestant, male and female, and even believer and unbeliever together now for worship and a common life for some fifty years.[4] It has helped a great many people to see again the importance of worship in the daily round, to have a more balanced view of the Christian life as a holistic ideal, and to renew their commitment to Christ in a way that sends them back into the world to serve those in need.

The fundamental sphere of Christian community, however, will always be in ordinary life in the secular world, and not in the life of a small group that withdraws from it. At best, the latter can be only a sign of and for the wider world, and for the possibilities of faith and life generally. If the Christian calling is supremely to love, then Christian love must come to be expressed where it matters most: in families, at work, in friendships, and even — dare we say it in a world so recently resurgent with right-wing politics? — in the sphere of the state. And here we find something of key significance for the church's role in the world. Western Christians have grown so accustomed to the idea that the social influence of the Christian churches is on the wane that we can scarcely see any longer the positive potential that lies dormant in our new situation. Church and society are no longer coterminous, or even nearly so. Typically, this fact has led to a certain despair in ecclesiastical circles. But in fact, the distance that now lies between church and world actually frees the church to be a sign to the world. Precisely because it is something other, something even somewhat "strange," the church can become what it is intended to be: "salt" and "light," a city set on a hill that all around can see — in fact, a sign and model of the kingdom of God. But it can only ever be so if love is seen as the "greatest of these," and if the contemporary drain within the church toward the worldly

4. An excellent introduction to the Iona Community can be found in Ron Fergusson, *George MacLeod: Founder of the Iona Community* (London: Collins, 1990).

values of individualism are checked by the demands of charity and by a sense of vocation in serving the needs of the neighbor and the glory of God.

Sanctity

The Christian calling has implications that extend well beyond the world of employment; in fact, we may say that *employment*, narrowly conceived, is the least of its concerns. Fundamentally, we are called to fellowship with God. Because God is love, this will always involve fellowship with other human beings as well. But it is God who matters supremely, and it is love for God that is first of all and above all commanded in Jesus' teaching. Many Christians nowadays are not used to what this might mean; we have grown so accustomed to hearing the gospel as a message of justice or peace, on the one hand, or as a message about personal salvation, on the other, that any message about love for God as the core of everything sounds strange to our ears. And yet, for most of Christian history, "the chief end of man," as the Westminster Shorter Catechism once eloquently put it, has been "to know God and enjoy him forever." The whole of time and eternity are thus to be spent in the love of God.

The word "sanctity," with which I have chosen to conclude this discussion, corresponds to this God-centered concern. Sanctity means holiness, and to be holy in the Bible is to be set apart, not for service as such, but simply for God. In the Old Testament, for example, even the inanimate things used in worship in the Temple became holy by being "sanctified," set apart for the worship of God. Holiness always involves a certain discrimination. Someone is seen as no longer simply immersed in the common affairs of the life of the world. The person takes on a new status: he or she belongs to God. It involves a transfer of status from one thing to another, from secular to sacred, from earth to heaven, or, more commonly in the New Testament, from unbelief to faith, from sin to righteousness. The translation from the one to the other also involves a paradoxical dynamic of detachment from the world on the one side and of service to the world on the other. No one can be bound in love to God without being concerned for God alone; and yet no one can love God, and above all God alone, without also loving the neighbor for whom Christ was sent by the Father and for whom he died. Thus the "one thing" that is "needful" (Luke 10:42, RSV) serves both to set one apart from common things and yet also to immerse one in them for the sake of others.

Strictly speaking, only God is holy. In the language of an older type of Christian theology, holiness is one of his "essential attributes." That is, it belongs to the definition of his being to be holy; God is not God without it. Therefore, holiness in the strict sense is something that only God can possess, for it is what he is. The creature cannot, therefore, be holy in the truest sense, even by way of derivation from God's essence, or by way of participation in the divine. When we speak of a holy man, or of a holy angel, or even of a holy sacrament or a holy day, we speak improperly, for only God is holy. Holiness is, therefore, a function of the "Godness of God."

Yet the commandment of God himself is this: "Be holy, for I am holy" (Lev. 11:44); because holiness defines the character of God, it is also to define the character of his people. In the first instance, this signifies a moral imperative. The purity of God is incompatible with sin. The Johannine tradition speaks of this in terms of light and darkness: "God is light and in him there is no darkness at all. If we say that we have fellowship with him while we are walking in darkness, we lie and do not do what is true" (1 John 1:5-6). The alternative is to "walk in the light," to "do what is true." But the holiness of God's people

122

is also something that pertains to their very being, their constitution as the people of God. In Christianity, holiness is seen to be the result of incorporation into Christ, the "holy one of God" (Luke 4:34), who "became for us wisdom from God, and righteousness and sanctification and redemption" (1 Cor. 1:30). The two aspects are brought together in a well-known text from 1 Peter 2:4-5: "Come to him, a living stone, though rejected by mortals yet chosen and precious in God's sight, and like living stones, let yourselves be built into a spiritual house, to be a holy priesthood, to offer spiritual sacrifices acceptable to God through Jesus Christ."

Here, there is more than enough to sustain a Christian theology of vocation, for the task is to be holy where we are, amid the responsibilities of ordinary life, and within the community or communities in which we live. Or, as a rather different theological source puts it, "Life in the Holy Spirit fulfils the vocation of man" (Catechism of the Catholic Church, 1699). Everything else must be secondary to this or, better, a function of it. To be "for God" in life — this constitutes the Christian doctrine of vocation. Such a life will take a variety of forms. It must be so, for the Christian vocation is a response to God, and the human response is constituted as much by the specific character of each person as by the general call of God to faith and obedience. "What does God call *me* to do?" is a question that nobody but I can answer. But the specific nature of each response, and the ensuing variety of Christian vocations, must not be allowed to cloud the fact that the fundamental structure of the Christian calling is the same in each case: the call is to the love of God, and because God is love, to the love of one's neighbor. What remains is to find the way of doing this that corresponds best to what lies in the self, to one's special gifts and qualities, within the specific circumstances of one's life. More than this cannot be done, and nothing more than this can be required of us.

CHAPTER 8

Choosing

A Parable

There was once a banker, a successful man in business for over thirty years. He worked as a senior administrator in a national bank in the south of England. The banker was also a husband and father, but not a terribly successful one. However competent and admired he may have been at work, at home he was a difficult person, irritable and often intolerant of his wife and especially of his children during their teens. They for their part tended to keep their distance from him. The banker-father was a source of wealth but not of love, and little love was shown in return.

Then at sixty, the banker took early retirement. Returning home after his last day at work, he was heard by his youngest son to say, "Thank God that's over! I've hated every f——g day of it!" The youngest son heard his words, astonished not so much at the language as at the sentiments expressed. None of the children had previously had any idea that their father was so unhappy with his work. Every appearance during the whole of their childhood had been that he was a workaholic banking

executive, totally dedicated to life at the office and little inter-
ested in spending time with his family. He seemed a man with
a mind only for money and power.

The children were, however, mistaken. Following retirement, the man's character was transformed. He became less
irritable, more tolerant, and happier within himself and within
the home generally. What surprised them equally was what he
did next. The father came from the upper-middle classes in the
south of England and belonged to a generation and a culture
for which there was little mixing between professionals and
manual workers. He had, in fact, gone into banking because it
was "what one did" in his family and in his day. Following
retirement, however, he opened a small carpenter's shop in his
garage. For the next ten years, he worked away contentedly for
small sums, repairing furniture and doing occasional odd jobs
about the community. His neighbors saw him as an eccentric,
but his wife and children welcomed the change. Over time, the
father and his mature sons became friends rather than acquain-
tances.

This serves as a warning: an occupation can be a destruc-
tive influence upon one's life, even though it may seem one's
destined lot. In particular, income may be a relatively unimportant factor in determining overall happiness. It is true that
for some people, having an important role in society and
"making a contribution" at some socially advanced level can be
something of great personal significance. On the other hand,
an occupation that allows a person to "get ahead" in such a
way can also make it difficult to live charitably or to have inner
peace of mind. A lack of adjustment to the social and economic
worlds can turn a person into someone he or she does not wish
to be. Social pressures, which in this case dictated that a man
from a middle-class family living in a "stock-broker belt" become a banker *rather than* a carpenter (perish the thought!),
ruined much of his life, and the lives of those for whom, after

all, he really cared. When a simpler way of life was chosen and the high-pressure world of money and power was left behind, he was more able to be the person he wanted to be.

Vocation and Career Choice

Although our theology of Christian vocation is now essentially complete, it is well to remind ourselves of stories such as these. This is especially so since the tale of the banker is more than a parable; it is a true story. How, then, does this theology of vocation relate to lives such as his? First of all, I have suggested that the Christian vocation is essentially to a life of faith and love. On this basis, the doctrine of vocation has been dissociated from the question of career choice. Much unhelpful psychological tension and religious confusion have been generated by the idea that God has a blueprint precisely tailored to each individual, extending down to the details of a working life. Second, however, this does not mean that there is *no* relation between work and vocation. In the case of the banker, for example, a working life appears effectively to have stood for thirty years between a man and his vocation.

The question "What will I do with my life?" is one that we must all face at some human level. It can arise at various stages of life, whenever decisions concerning the future must be made. Especially at crucial turning points, sometimes during periods of deep disquiet and uncertainty, the question can be very acute indeed. How, then, can we answer it? Without wishing to disappoint, I have to say that the short answer is that within the broad framework of the Christian vocation to faith and love, with all that this involves, it does not matter greatly. One does not disobey God by choosing any one worthwhile secular occupation over another, or by retiring at sixty rather than at sixty-five. The longer answer, however, must be

126

one that is able to take account of the specific circumstances, abilities, and opportunities available to the individual, that is flexible enough to accommodate differences in personality, and that is able to see all of this as morally and theologically meaningful.

Ours is an age of freedom, but our freedom is both blessing and curse. We hold within ourselves the potential not only for personal fulfillment and liberation but also for personal disaster and disappointment. Hence we find the responsibility of choice a terrifying thing. If only there were a cosmic plan to which we had access, dictating the ideal path by which we could negotiate the obstacles of life! In the light of the responsibilities of choosing, some people will perhaps wish that there were still hereditary occupations and more stable social norms dictating the path or paths to be taken in life. Others still turn to the cycles of the stars! But these are no longer real options for us. The truth is that the human struggle involved in such decisions today is pervasive and virtually unavoidable.

It is human freedom that makes such decisions ethical in their character. It is only because we have a choice, and to the extent that we have a choice, that such personal and moral dilemmas about the future arise. In the most fundamental sense, they concern what the *ethos,* the character of our lives is to be, if not questions of good and evil per se. This point is important. Very often, the choices available will, from the standpoint of what we might describe as "flat" moral criteria, be equally attractive. In fact, were they not, the alternatives would not be valid alternatives; immoral decisions must be excluded. Still, however, I could have two children or three, retire early or work on, or choose to become either a teacher or a carpenter. No one could say conclusively that one of these alternatives was in and of itself any more virtuous than the other. But the choice will certainly bear upon the life and character of the person making the decision: it makes a great deal of difference in a home and to a parent whether two or three children are present, and unhappiness may well result from an inappropriate choice of career, however valuable and legitimate the work may be in itself.

Virtue Theory and Religious Knowledge

There is a whole school of moral thought known as "virtue theory" that relates to such matters, according to which the appropriate question for us to ask in much of ethics is not primarily "What ought I to do?" but rather "What sort of person ought I to be?" Certain options can be ruled out in advance — that is, those that are obviously immoral. But many ethical questions have less to do with specific actions than with the question of individual character and social structures. This line of moral thought is associated in particular with the names of Alasdair MacIntyre in moral philosophy and Stanley Hauerwas in Christian ethics, but it also has deep roots in ancient Greek philosophy and is defended by a range of contemporary moral theorists.[1]

MacIntyre is perhaps the most important representative of such thinking in recent times. His moral theory is developed in a number of works spanning some years, but for our purposes the key text is his book *After Virtue*.[2] MacIntyre's position is developed first of all in the light of the breakdown of the classical Christian worldview as the norm in Western society,

1. An overview is provided by Greg Pence, "Virtue Theory," in *A Companion to Ethics,* ed. Peter Singer (Oxford: Blackwell, 1993), pp. 249-58; see also the superb treatment provided by Jean Porter, *The Recovery of Virtue* (Louisville: Westminster/John Knox Press, 1990).

2. Alasdair MacIntyre, *After Virtue* (Notre Dame: University of Notre Dame Press, 1981).

and second in the light of the fact that there is no single rationally convincing account possible regarding which concrete actions are good and which are evil in any given case. For MacIntyre, there always has been and always will be diversity of opinion about such things, so that the Enlightenment ideal of a single human morality, known by reason, proves to be unworkable in the pragmatic sense. Furthermore, MacIntyre insists, the Enlightenment's rational ideals have broken down in twentieth-century thought and must be abandoned in moral theory on philosophical grounds. In place of such a rationalistic moral vision, and ostensibly drawing on the philosophy of Aristotle (p. 201), MacIntyre wishes to substitute an ethical view built on an attempt to integrate narrative theory into moral theory. The nature of the moral good is an extremely complex subject, but what we must say about it, according to MacIntyre, is that its fundamental referent is human life, and that human life is best understood, not through abstract definition or logical analysis, but through narrative. When we try to understand ourselves, in other words, we tell stories: I was born in such and such a place, had such and such experiences and opportunities, made such and such decisions on the basis of information available, and so on. MacIntyre's basic claim is that there is no alternative to such a narrative procedure in attempting to comprehend the moral life. It can be understood, and expressed, only in narrative terms.

For our purposes, what is most important about such virtue theory is that what constitutes a life story is unity, and since a life story is something told about years of living, unity in such a story implies that it has some direction, some "point." There are obviously certain constants in anyone's life story: one cannot change one's physical parentage, for example, or avoid the need for nutrition and sleep. Education is gained within the limits of what is economically and physically available. Not everything, then, is within our choice. Much of our development, and much of the narrative we build up around it and by which we interpret it, is simply a "given." But along with this passive aspect, there is a more active process by which our personal stories are built up. We constitute ourselves, in a very real sense, to the extent that we *do* make certain decisions concerning the course of our lives. A person theoretically has the potential to live any number of lives within the limits available, and so to "tell" any number of stories. According to MacIntyre, however, for a human life to have meaning it must be capable of being expressed in a single story, a single narrative with a sense of continuity, which has direction, a *telos* or goal (pp. 217-18). Clearly, the choice of career will be among the major factors affecting the content of the emerging narrative.

Virtue theory has an obvious application to the religious aspects of career choice. First of all, it presupposes that the rightness or wrongness of any given decision to pursue a particular career relates primarily, not to the career itself, but to the character and potential of the person concerned. Our basic question in deciding between two equally attractive and ethically acceptable occupations does not really concern the moral value associated with the choice of one of the two occupations; rather, it concerns the sort of person one wishes to be, the way in which one chooses to live, and the sense of fulfillment that may or may not follow on one choice as opposed to the other. I am less certain about MacIntyre's insistence on "narratability" as the core concern in the moral life, partly because (as he himself admits) an intelligible account of a life must be made in terms of some generally accepted set of criteria as to what constitutes a life of virtue, or even a socially acceptable form of employment. There is a sense, therefore, in which virtue theory depends, paradoxically, upon a general theory of virtue — which is just what that position set out in the beginning to avoid. The intelligibility of the narrative developed will also depend heavily on other factors, such as what it is possible for a given individual to do within the limits of his or her physical resources or the physical resources of the state. Were a semi-literate agricultural peasant from Asia to tell us of her ambition to become an astronaut, we would shake our heads in disbelief, but the same would not necessarily be our response in similar circumstances to a young American with her heart set on training to be a Navy test pilot.

In one important respect, however, the idea of narratability does offer a valuable insight into how a religious person might go about making a career choice. A narrative is an artistic form of discourse, whether the narrative be in the form of a written biography or in the form of a simple story told privately. This suggests that making choices concerning one's future may be more akin to the production of a work of art than to making a straightforward moral decision between good and evil. In art, there is no one "right answer"; instead, there are alternative visions of the beautiful and of the good (in drama, for example), visions that are intended as much or more to open up new possibilities as to provide an objective account of the world. There are innumerable portraits of people, young and old, but what makes them works of beauty is notoriously hard to say. Similarly, there are literary works in which the moral qualities of the hero strike alternative readers very differently: Is Shakespeare's *Hamlet* a straightforward tragedy or a comedy of sorts? To answer such questions, one has to develop a sense of judgment, a way of feeling as well as of thinking, which goes far beyond the application of formal rules of logic or scientific method.

Religious knowledge generally is very similar to aesthetic appreciation. Admittedly, there are hard "facts" that one can absorb, such as the names of the books of the Bible or of the Apostles. Even the content of the Bible or of the creeds can be assimilated as sheer information. Having such knowledge would not, however, mean that the content in either case would yet be *understood* in the religious sense. Religious life is about participation in the primordial mystery of God through prayer, worship, and lifestyle, all of which involves so much more than bare knowledge. Religion relates to fundamental issues of life and death, to what it is to be a human being, and to what it is to live in relationship to God. There are few, if any, technical, total answers to the questions religion asks. In fact, its answers are generally badly misunderstood if they are seen as much more than means by which the all-encompassing mystery of God can be glimpsed and grasped in fragments.

In a recent study in the psychology of religion, Fraser Watts and Mark Williams have drawn attention to the parallels between the processes of self-knowledge in view in psychological analysis and the processes by which religious believers come to a grasp of the content of religious teaching.[3] They are also critical of the widespread tendency in much philosophy of religion, and in philosophical theology in particular, to draw parallels between scientific and religious knowledge on the grounds that all scientific data are really theory-laden. On this view, there is no such thing as a scientific "fact," pure and simple. In a similar way, it is often argued, there is no such thing as religious experience in and for itself: religious experience, like everything else, is *interpreted* experience. Since interpretation is a constant feature in all human experience, religious experience is as legitimate a form of experience as any other, scientific experience included (pp. 50-51). One cannot, therefore, rule out the legitimacy of religious experience on scientific-positivist grounds, since such a procedure is actually inconsistent with the foundations of science itself.

Watts and Williams criticize this view on the grounds that the issue in religious knowledge, seen from the standpoint of

3. Fraser Watts and Mark Williams, *The Psychology of Religious Knowing* (Cambridge: Cambridge University Press, 1988).

the psychological processes involved, is not purely cognitive or theoretical. Instead, religious knowledge is more like what can only be called personal knowledge or the knowledge of the heart — the knowledge one has of the self or of some significant "other" in life. As psychologists, they draw particular attention to the parallel between religious knowing and psychotherapeutic knowledge (pp. 70-74). Both involve emotional life as much as or even more, at times, than cognition. Both are concerned with a movement from insight to personal transformation. Mere knowledge is of little moral or therapeutic value; as we are told in holy Scripture, the demons also believe — and tremble (James 2:19). In both cases, we are frequently brought face to face with symbolism. Symbolic ideas can be merely the tips of icebergs, which loom up massively in the light from far beneath the surface on closer approach. In both cases, there is a synthesis of what is objective and what is subjective and an attempt to transcend the crude dichotomy frequently posited between them. If this is true, however, then the conditions that apply to the acquisition of psychotherapeutic insight will, prima facie, apply also to the acquisition of religious insight: insight is predicated upon openness. In both spheres, we need "to look beyond what is obvious and what it is convenient to acknowledge" in order to achieve the insight we require (p. 152).

Knowledge, in fact, is not necessarily central to religious life at all. In many traditions, religious life is seen as a path of "unknowing," a way of living in relation to the infinite that refuses detailed classification, formulae, and answers. This is certainly true of the Christian mystical tradition, with its emphasis on the "negative way" of approach to God. Insofar as one persists in saying what God is, in short, one has not yet grasped that God is beyond all categories. In the teaching of Jesus, furthermore, it is love rather than knowledge that is especially important and serves as the chief characteristic of the new relationship with God that he proclaims, while the wise and learned tend to be excluded. He does not ask us to follow him in an abstract theology, but in obedience and devotion, in service and faith. As I have pointed out, even the word "theology" itself, as the *logos* of *theos,* can readily mislead at this point, especially if, through an emphasis on knowing, a particular theological approach effectively excludes the moral, relational, and mystical aspects of religious life from the center of its vision.

The Struggle

How, then, do we choose a career? The truth is that there is sometimes no easy answer to a question that can run so deep. The philosopher Dorothy Emmett, in a treatment of the idea of vocation, once drew attention to a student who had been commended to her on the basis of the results of psychometric assessment: "his measured interests on a standardized vocational interest test are definitely in the general social science field, with superior measured interest in the following fields: teaching, clergyman, personnel psychology and social service, with 94 percentile measured interest maturity."[4] Her response is illuminating: what is called vocational guidance ought to reckon more closely with individual people.

Individual people usually struggle with the question of career choice. The adolescent, encouraged, perhaps, by a fond parent, may well have a set view of what the future holds, but the transition to adulthood often brings into play serious doubts about formerly cherished ambitions. The young man who decides to marry, similarly, will inevitably reflect carefully on his choice of partner, but he will most likely be able to carry

4. Dorothy Emmet, *Function, Purpose and Powers,* 2nd ed. (London: Macmillan, 1972), p. 243.

through with his commitment only in fear and trembling — sometimes quite literally at the altar on the "day of reckoning." Doubt is oftentimes a necessary ingredient in the quest for certainty, doubt that arises "out of the depths," *de profundis*.

Such considerations are prominent in a recent study by the Canadian philosopher James Horne, in which the relevance of mysticism to the question of career choice is highlighted.[5] Horne notes that the typical experience of the mystic in the Christian tradition (among others) involves a path through darkness into light. The darkness is a necessary stage within the whole journey of spiritual development. Horne attempts to draw a parallel between such mystical experience and the psychological processes by which individuals make decisions concerning their future. There is, he suggests, much to be gained from such an analysis. The feeling of being "at sea," and even of lacking an integrated self-image and of wishing to have one, is common currency in many young people's experience. We cannot choose for the future without a sense of identity in the present and without a realistic sense of what we may become. Horne's treatment of mysticism and vocation allows us to understand this as a necessary part of the process by which such a decision is made — to give it a name, to "baptize" the apparent meaninglessness as something religiously and psychologically necessary. Yet the essential thing for those who wrestle with career choice in such an existential way is finally to transcend the darkness in such a way as to lay plans for the future, to have a project in life.

One must, of course, distinguish between what is theoretically possible and what is pragmatically possible, between the tentative decisions made at some earlier stage in life and what actually becomes possible on the basis of decisions already

5. James R. Horne, *Mysticism and Vocational Choice* (Waterloo: Wilfred Laurier University Press, 1996).

made. I may wish to work at such and such an occupation in some geographical area; in the event, I may be able to realize the first ambition, but not the second. I may even discover as life goes on that the second rather than the first ambition was closer to my heart. It may be that living "in exile" will be what pains me most about my circumstances as I mature; my children, for example, may thus grow up without knowing their grandparents. A sense of place, of location in the world, can be extremely important, whereas the working role assumed is less important. The potential variety of factors to consider is enormous, so much so that, in the final analysis, there is no escaping the conclusion that any career choice will inevitably be a risky venture, undertaken "in faith," or in a kind of faith, in relation to what is as yet unseen and unknown.

Vocation and Mission

For the Christian, however, the decisive consideration is that a life project must be capable of being integrated into the overall mission of Christ. Christ's mission is a mission of love, of self-giving service, and of obedience to God. My argument has been that the question "What ought I to do?" really leads to another: "What kind of person ought I to be?" There is no clear answer to the first — insofar, at least, as it is a question concerned solely with career choice. However, much clearer answers can be given to the second question. I ought to be a person for whom love, service, and obedience to God are the major priorities. The Christian ethic is flexible insofar as it allows a multitude of possibilities by which one can fulfill such goals, but there is nevertheless an irreducible core concern within it, which can never be relinquished.

Let me illustrate this by outlining three possible paths that I might have taken in life. The first option requires some reference to my own family background. For centuries my ancestors have made a living from the sea. I also might have done so. I come from a region in which the fishing industry is a major source of wealth, and in which there were opportunities for a young man such as I was when I left school. Had I become a fisherman, my life would certainly have been very different from what it is today. I would, for example, most probably have remained a member of the local community within which I was born and grew up and thus maintained the link between my family and that place, a link that has lasted (until now) for some three centuries. The friends of youth would have remained the friends of adult life, and I would have been at hand for my aging parents. The commandment to honor one's father and mother would have been fulfilled in this way. I would also have been able to maintain contact with people and with a place that I love. No doubt there would have been opportunities to become involved locally in community and church work. I would have taken up a useful role in relation to the rest of society, providing food for others. Had I married and raised a family, I could have shown love in that context; the monotony of early mornings and days at sea would have been offset by the knowledge that a family was cared for. My Christian faith would no doubt have remained simpler than it is now, for I would probably have read little theology, but this would not have been a great burden or hindrance to my fulfillment, which would have come in other ways. I am, in fact, attracted to such a life still, punctuated as it is by the rhythm of the seasons and based as it is on strong ties with the sea and the land.

Would any of this been incompatible with sharing in the mission of Christ? I do not think so. Some of it would have been much more compatible with it than the path I finally took in life. For one surely owes a debt to one's own society and people, to those, for example, who provided an education, and to the Christian community that nurtured one's faith. The people whose lives might have been affected by my own were very much as real in that world as they are in my situation today. And for me, an especially important consideration is that my own father would not have died while I worked far away.

Another alternative was available. I might well have gone into business. Suppose, for the sake of argument, that the business had been successful and that I had gone on to build up a modest company which, after twenty years, employed twenty people and looked set to make me modestly wealthy. Would this have been compatible with the mission of Christ? The answer, I believe, is yes — especially in my home context. In resource-based economies, there is often insufficient secondary industry. The result is that there is much unemployment and sometimes surprising poverty. In such a context, the creation of wealth in business would have been more than self-service or worship at the altar of greed, even were such sins a factor in the whole story. For the creation of wealth can be the creation of new possibilities for an entire community, with prospects of work for young people and a prosperity that enables social as well as economic well-being. For a few people, at least, the cycle of welfare dependency might have been broken. Economic prospects can generate hope as well as wealth, sustaining communities and helping people to live a full life. And along the way, opportunities for service, for living in love within a family, or for participating constructively in the life of a Christian congregation would also have been present.

In the event, of course, I became a scholar. Contrary to my own expectation, which was that I would enter the Christian ministry and work with my own people in a pastoral way, I was drawn more and more deeply into academic issues and into an academic culture far from my original goals. It has been a surprising journey for me, going against my own plans at a number of crucial junctures. However, I find that the needs of my neighbor are much the same here as elsewhere, and that the so-called "ivory tower" of higher education has as much genuine reality in it as does any other sphere of life. As well as the usual grind that is the warp and woof of most occupations, ample opportunities for serving others and even for preaching and pastoral care arise. In the meantime, I have a wife and family, and within the home I am sustained and I help to sustain other human lives in dignity and in love.

Which of the three paths "ought" I to have taken? There is no clear answer to such a question, for there is no clear moral imperative governing the situation. In each case, the opportunity to participate in one way or another in the mission of Christ was open to me. I would go further, in fact, and say that it was *equally* open to me under any of the scenarios presented, for there is nothing especially saintly about my present work as a theologian, nothing intrinsic to it to lift it beyond the possibility of self-centeredness or faithlessness. The calling to be faithful and loving is one that extends to any and all walks of life and that cannot be identified with any one of them. And it is this calling to faithfulness and love with which Christian vocation is really concerned, the calling to follow the one who obeyed the Father to the end, who laid down his life for his friends — the one who, as such, was raised from the dead and exalted to the right hand of the Father.

The Way of Life

Psychological studies have demonstrated that people with a clear sense of direction are often also more integrated as persons.[6] It is only what might be expected, though one has to add to this the qualification that some who *appear* to be most

6. Edmund Bourne, "The State of Research on Ego Identity: A Review and Appraisal," *Journal of Youth and Adolescence* 7 (1978): 223-51, 371-91.

certain are also sometimes the most vulnerable should doubts about their chosen path ever arise. Nevertheless, there is a sense in which one constantly lives, and can only live, with a view to the future, to what one may become. Only thus can one be a full human being. The acorn becomes an oak, and in the same way the youth becomes an adult, while adulthood brings with it special opportunities and responsibilities; the adult, finally, grows old, enters into a period of retirement, and at last dies. Life itself is organic, being fundamentally characterized by growth and movement. Religious life is similar: one of the pervasive metaphors found within it is the "journey," the "pilgrimage," by which one travels along life's way into the light and love of God. Here as elsewhere, without such orientation to the future life itself would be inconceivable.

The philosopher Aristotle, who saw the entire universe in such developmental terms, once observed that we are likely to develop to our full potential only if we have sight of our goal. Like archers who have a mark to aim at, it is obviously more likely that we will hit the target if we can actually see it than if we do not.[7] Aristotle himself construed the goal of human life as happiness, by which he meant a general state of well-being corresponding to the fulfillment of various aspects of "natural" human potentiality, rather than a purely emotional state. He then went on to develop a moral philosophy of the virtues — that is, those qualities "by virtue of which" a person can attain to the human goal. Thus the human acorn becomes the adult oak. There is, I believe, a great deal of truth in this. A life is "full" to the extent that a person has reached a goal that is appropriate to a human being, and to this extent such a person will achieve "happiness" in the sense of well-being. What is entirely missing from Aristotle's account of the moral life, however, is any reference to the human relation to God as

7. Aristotle, *Nicomachean Ethics,* 1094a, 24.

the context of such development. And at this point, I want to say, his position is badly flawed.

Jesus speaks of the human goal in two ways. The first is in terms of the great commandments. The human goal and the divine imperative here coalesce: "you shall love the Lord your God with all your heart . . . ; you shall love your neighbor as yourself" (Mark 12:30-31 par.). From the standpoint of the spiritual life, the human goal is succinctly summed up in these key statements. The second, and literally crucial way in which Jesus speaks of the goal of life is in terms of discipleship: "If any want to become my followers, let them deny themselves and take up their cross and follow me" (Mark 8:34 par.). According to this teaching, we find life by relinquishing it, by sacrificing our small goods to the overriding good of the gospel of the kingdom and for the sake of the name of Christ. I have chosen the title *The Way of Life* for this book with this in view: the "way of life," according to the Christian gospel, is a paradoxical "way" that involves self-denial and often leads through suffering. There is no other "way," in this sense, to our goal. Nevertheless, within this one "way" are a multiplicity of individual paths that we tread. But we navigate by means of the same signs, following the same rules, living one life of love and discipleship.

At the beginning of this book, I wrote of my own childish belief that God had a plan for each life, a plan that a given individual might miss if he or she was not attentive to God's call and obedient to his voice. As a youth, I took such a view. It was as if I were waiting for a bus, or a "streetcar named vocation"; if I became bored and decided to wander away from the street, it would pass me by. But is it really possible to miss the will of God in this way? I have found such a vision of the Christian vocation to be extremely unhelpful, and because I am convinced that there are many people (especially young people) who are similarly mistaken, I have sought to develop a different understanding of the Christian vocation. Christian

141

vocation is not reducible to the acquisition of a career goal or to its realization in time. It is, rather, something relating to the great issues of the spiritual life. It has to do with what one lives "for" rather than with what one does.

Such an understanding, once developed, can liberate us from the tyranny of such notions as the one that some have vocations whereas others do not, from the idea that having a vocation is incompatible with being unemployed or retired, from despair over not being able to "hear" God's voice when looking into the future at turning points in life. The human vocation is to do the will of God and so to live life "abundantly" (John 10:10), but the will of God does not extend down to the details of career choice. And once this is realized, I believe, then it becomes possible for us to live more adventurously, more freely, breathing in an atmosphere of love rather than law, looking for *our own* way to share the good news of the gospel in daily life, whether in career choices or in business or in the ordinary transactions of the daily round. Here, new possibilities open for the creating of Christian lifestyle and modes of spirituality that reflect the generosity of God in Christ. For this, at heart, is the Christian's vocation.

Select Bibliography

Balthasar, Hans Urs von. *The Christian State of Life.* Translated by Sister Mary Frances McCarthy. San Francisco: Ignatius Press, 1983.

————. *Theo-Drama,* vol. III. Translated by Graham Harrison. San Francisco: Ignatius Press, 1992.

Barth, Karl. *Church Dogmatics,* IV/2. Edited by T. F. Torrance and G. W. Bromiley. Translated by G. W. Bromiley. Edinburgh: T. & T. Clark, 1962.

Beardslee, William A. *Human Achievement and Divine Vocation in the Message of Paul.* London: SCM Press, 1961.

Fichter, Joseph H. *Religion as an Occupation: A Study in the Sociology of Professions.* Notre Dame: University of Notre Dame Press, 1966.

Forrester, William R. *Christian Vocation: Studies in Faith and Work.* London: Lutterworth Press, 1951.

Hardy, Lee. *The Fabric of This World: Inquiries into Calling, Career Choice, and the Design of Human Work.* Grand Rapids: Wm. B. Eerdmans Publishing Co., 1990.

Horne, James R. *Mysticism and Vocational Choice.* Waterloo: Wilfred Laurier University Press, 1996.

Oswald, Roy M., and Otto Kroeger. *Personality Type and Religious Leadership*. Washington, DC: Alban Institute, 1988.

Shaw, Robert B. *The Call of God: The Theme of Vocation in the Poetry of Donne and Herbert*. Cambridge, MA: Cowley Publications, 1981.

Speyr, Adrienne von. *They Followed His Call: Vocation and Asceticism*. Revised edition. Translated by Erasmo Leiva-Merikakis. San Francisco: Ignatius Press, 1986.

Volf, Miroslav. *Work in the Spirit: Toward a Theology of Work*. New York: Oxford University Press, 1991.

Watts, Fraser, and Mark Williams. *The Psychology of Religious Knowing*. Cambridge: Cambridge University Press, 1988.

Wingren, Gustav. *Luther on Vocation*. Translated by Carl C. Rasmussen. Philadelphia: Muhlenberg Press, 1957. (Also published under the title *The Christian's Calling: Luther on Vocation*. Edinburgh: Oliver and Boyd, 1958.)

Index

146